Henry Weyland Chetwynd

Three hundred a year

Vol. I

Henry Weyland Chetwynd

Three hundred a year
Vol. I

ISBN/EAN: 9783337040918

Printed in Europe, USA, Canada, Australia, Japan

Cover: Foto ©ninafisch / pixelio.de

More available books at **www.hansebooks.com**

THREE HUNDRED A YEAR.

A Novel.

BY THE HON.

Mrs. HENRY WEYLAND CHETWYND.

IN TWO VOLUMES.

VOL. I.

LONDON:
TINSLEY BROTHERS, CATHERINE STREET, STRAND.
1866.

TO

CAPTAIN THE HON.

HENRY WEYLAND CHETWYND, R.N.,

This Book is Dedicated,

BY HIS AFFECTIONATE WIFE,

JULIA B. CHETWYND.

CONTENTS

OF

THE FIRST VOLUME.

CHAPTER		PAGE
I.	LOVE, MATRIMONY, AND GENERAL GOSSIP	1
II.	BERTHA'S FATE IS SETTLED	14
III.	MISS THURSTON REMONSTRATES WITHOUT EFFECT	18
IV.	LADY HAUGHTON THINKS SHE MUST INTERFERE	25
V.	LADY HAUGHTON TURNS DIPLOMATIST	32
VI.	IN WHICH SIR LUKE HAUGHTON'S CHARACTER IS DISCUSSED	37
VII.	THE OTHER UNCLE	42
VIII.	MATRIMONIAL	59
IX.	MUNDANE MATTERS	63
X.	FRANK HERBERT BUYS EXPENSIVE THINGS, STRICTLY ON PHILOSOPHICAL PRINCIPLES	69
XI.	BREAKERS AHEAD!	75
XII.	FRANK HERBERT TRIES TO SEE HIS WAY	85
XIII.	TROUBLED WATERS	91
XIV.	THE FRIENDLY LAWYER	99
XV.	KNOWING THE WORST	118

CONTENTS.

CHAPTER		PAGE
XVI.	THE TANGLED SKEIN UNRAVELLED	126
XVII.	CHANGE OF SCENE	134
XVIII.	A MODEL RECTOR	145
XIX.	A NEW LIGHT ON THE SUBJECT OF CLERICAL DUTIES	156
XX.	"SCHEIDEN, SCHEIDEN TUT WEH!"	164
XXI.	TROUBLES AND TRIALS	174
XXII.	REFLECTIONS	182
XXIII.	HOMEWARD BOUND	189
XXIV.	"HOME! SWEET HOME!"	200
XXV.	M. LE COMTE VON PEFFERSTEIN	206
XXVI.	FRANK HERBERT BECOMES SANGUINE	215
XXVII.	ANOTHER MOVE	221
XXVIII.	BERTHA RENEWS ACQUAINTANCE WITH SOME OF HER RELATIONS AND FRIENDS	229
XXIX.	LADY CECIL	236
XXX.	COUSINS	245
XXXI.	BERTHA SEES LONDON UNDER NEW AUSPICES	255
XXXII.	THE DUCHESS OF BRANLINGHAM	260
XXXIII.	COMMON SENSE	268
XXXIV.	ABROAD	272
XXXV.	MADAME LA PRINCESSE DE SAUERLICH	282
XXXVI.	THE TOWN OF DESSELDRINGEN AND ITS FAVOURITE PHYSICIAN	289
XXXVII.	A HUNT BALL	297

THREE HUNDRED A YEAR.

CHAPTER I.

LOVE, MATRIMONY, AND GENERAL GOSSIP.

"How I do hate those bells!" exclaimed Miss Priscilla Thurston, as she sat at work with her sister, in a small room of a small house in the village of Eppington. "Ring, ring, ring; never have they ceased this blessed afternoon—enough to drive one crazy!"

"They must leave off soon now," said her sister, a meek-looking little woman, with a depressed and faded air about her; "every one will be going to bed soon now."

"And such a cause for merriment, or bells!" continued the irate Miss Priscilla, paying no regard to the offered consolation; "a wedding! I never saw such a wedding. A bride! poor misguided young thing; marry in haste to repent at leisure; that's what she's done."

"Bertha has been engaged several months, and it has been a very long acquaintance," put in Miss Mary, gently.

"Long acquintance? nonsense!" rejoined Miss Priscilla, her cap, with its multifarious bows, vibrating energetically as she spoke; "how can you talk of a long acquaintance, when you know it was only a few months ago, in this very room, that Miss Haughton declared she scarcely knew him at all!"

"That was merely her way of speaking," answered Miss Mary; "and they have been engaged seven months and one fortnight, which is a tolerably long engagement. Surely, they may be supposed to know their own minds by this time!"

"As if," exclaimed Miss Priscilla, "any two people really knew each other better for being engaged, and did not play pretty to each other all the time."

"No one can accuse Mr. Herbert of playing pretty, as you call it," said Miss Mary. "He is particularly plain spoken, even to Bertha; he never goes out of his way to pay her the slightest compliment. He is——"

"He is the most disagreeable man I ever saw in my life," said Miss Priscilla, shortly, "and that is one reason why I cannot understand the marriage."

"He is desperately in love!" said her sister, glad to be able to advance one fact without fear of contradiction.

"Is he really?" rejoined Miss Priscilla, in a most irritating and sarcastic tone. "I thought most people were supposed to be 'in love' when they are fools enough to marry; but I am glad your sense of honesty is too strong for you to say *they* are. Miss Haughton is a perfect puzzle to me. I do not think she is one bit 'in love,' as you call it; and why she should go out of her way to marry a man who has positively nothing to recommend him—that is, according to *my* views," she added, grandly—" for he has neither looks, nor money, nor position, nor even talent. It is certainly a puzzle to me!"

"You do not do him justice," said Miss Mary; "you do not know him at all, really."

"You know him so much better!" retorted her sister. "He has met me twice, and contradicted me flatly both times. You have certainly met him oftener, so I suppose he has contradicted you so much oftener."

"You would talk upon a subject you really did not know much about, Priscilla," said her sister. "You began to talk about the discipline of the army——"

"I did," answered Miss Priscilla, solemnly; "and though you are so kind as to say I did not know my subject, and your intimate friend Mr. Herbert was so polite as to contradict me flatly, I beg to tell you I *have* studied the subject."

"You have read one short pamphlet, taking a very limited view of a very difficult question," said her sister, in a deprecating voice. "Mr. Herbert, as a soldier, of course was able to put you right. Practical knowledge——"

"Practical fiddlesticks!" said Miss Priscilla, who, according to the female instinct, got violent when she found herself in the wrong. "All I have to say is this, that if Miss Haughton had had either father or mother living, she never would have been allowed to make such a marriage; and as those bells have chosen to leave off at last, I am going to bed." So saying, she stalked off under the pleasing influence of having had the last word.

Miss Mary sat for some time after her sister's departure, quiet, grave, and not a little sad. She had been with Bertha all the morning, had accompanied her to the altar, and had seen her start from Haughton Hall, with Mr. Herbert. Not a misgiving had shaded a particularly bright face. She had no tears to shed, as she left no sisters or brothers, and had no father or mother to regret. Why should Miss Mary feel depressed except, as she told herself, a wedding was always a sad thing; and Mrs. Herbert's departure created a great blank in an already monotonous and colourless life.

Miss Priscilla had a knack of making her sister very unhappy at times; if Miss Mary indulged in a cap, and thought it becoming, Miss Priscilla would enlighten her on the subject, by telling her of a comical effect behind, which had the desired effect of shaking that confidence in her personal appearance which was a necessity to Miss Mary's peace of mind and general comfort. As in trifles, so it was in things of more moment, and the weaker sister, with a far wider experience of life, had never been far enough away from the blighting influence of her elder sister to acquire confidence in her own judgment. She had the habit of mistrusting herself. The wedding that had taken place that morning was one of the deepest interest to her. Sir Clement Haughton's only child had been her pupil from a very early age, and from the fact of being motherless, had grown up entirely dependent on Miss Mary Thurston for all womanly care, rewarding her by lavishing upon her the warm affection of a loving nature, and receiving in return the most untiring love, the most devoted watchfulness. Sir Clement's death had brought about their separation. Bertha, then eighteen, continued to live at Haughton with her uncle (now Sir Luke Haughton), and his wife, with children of her own, and more than one governess, saw no necessity for Miss Mary Thurston's continued residence. The grief of parting was lessened by her settling in the village close to the

Hall park gates, with her sister, both being independent—thanks to their own exertions. A few years passed away, and Bertha Haughton was twenty-three, and still Miss Bertha. The county had already speculated on various matrimonial engagements she was supposed to have entered into—when it was taken by surprise by the announcement of her intended marriage to a distant connexion of her own; a young man of no fortune, and, as far as was known, no prospects. True, his family was old, but it was impoverished; and he was the son of a younger son, and in the army.

Miss Mary Thurston was harassed by remarks, questions, and observations;—*she* was supposed to know the *ins* and *outs* of this marriage; was it Lady Haughton's arrangement? Lady Haughton's eldest daughter could not "come out" for some years, therefore her prospects and comforts could not be affected in any way by

Miss Bertha's remaining single; but it was possible that her ladyship had reasons . . It was well known Miss Bertha had money, but Eppington was too near the Hall to have false impressions on this subject, and it was not enough, in the opinion of any one near Haughton, to keep Miss Bertha in the style she had been accustomed to, and she was not considered fitted in any way to become what is called a "good poor man's wife."

"I mean no reflection on your training, my dear Miss Mary," said the gossiping mother of three plain daughters, to the poor little woman; "but when I paid my respects to the ladies at Haughton only a short time ago, I happened to mention that wonderful parrot, shaded from life by my eldest daughter, and was explaining all about the *hours* it took to make Polly sit for the correct putting in of the eyes,— Miss Haughton cut me short, in that independent way of hers, and said, it was very clever no doubt, but that she hated work, and did not know one end of a worsted needle from another. Now, for a wife who will probably have to see a good deal of her needle all her life, it's a bad look-out!"

"Miss Haughton works beautifully—plain work, I mean," said Miss Mary. "And she has, as you know, an off-hand way of talking; she does not expect to be taken literally."

"Well, if she works, no one knows when she does it," rejoined Mrs. Borewell. "She is never at home; scampering over the fields, hedges, and ditches, on that mild-looking horse, and driving her ponies, up and down hill, at the rate of twelve miles an hour. I have a great respect for all the Haughton family, my dear ma'am, a very *great* respect, but Miss Bertha has made a mistake, and we shall live to see it!"

This was the sort of conversation Miss

Mary had had to hear ever since Bertha's engagement had been announced, and she could meet it but feebly, oppressed by the conviction of its truth.

No one had remonstrated more earnestly than she had done with Bertha, though she did not choose to betray her feelings to her sister, or any one else. No one knew so well as she did how totally unfit Bertha was for the life she had chosen.

Careless in everything connected with money matters, Sir Clement had never given his daughter an allowance; he had never restricted her in any way. When she wanted money she was referred to his man of business, and got it. All she ordered was paid for in the same way; she never had a bill sent to her; and she had not the slightest idea of the value of money. Sir Clement left her 10,000*l*.; he had intended doing more, but he died before he was able to carry out his intentions. Miss

Mary thought now, sadly enough, over all she had said to Bertha, how often lately she had tried to persuade her that a certain amount of money was necessary to happiness, however much love there might be. Besides, Miss Mary, clear-sighted enough where Bertha's interests were in question, saw that in her case "love" was the pleasure of a devoted love *offered*, not the genuine, real love given; though Bertha, yearning for affection, mistook the gratitude of a nature craving for love—for the love itself.

All poor Miss Mary's remonstrances were received kindly, but with a feeling of calm superiority. Lounging over the fire in her dressing-room, Bertha dreamt of sacrifices, and declared poverty to be an ennobling virtue! Glancing over the bill of fare beside her plate at dinner (at which time the prolonged absence of a certain "crême glacée à la vanille" was acknowledged to be a grievance), the cookery of her future establishment never for one moment flitted across her imagination! In a dreamy way she talked of a future poverty, and gloried in the opportunity of proving how disinterested she was!

CHAPTER II.

BERTHA'S FATE IS SETTLED.

Lady Haughton was glad Bertha was going to marry; with a number of young children of her own, she had never cordially taken to her. Bertha frequently confessed, with a candour that was not flattering to her mother, that the children bored her, and her occasional appearance in society dragged Lady Haughton from her arm-chair, her novel, and her babies. If Bertha chose to marry a poor man, it was her own look-out; plenty of rich men would be glad to marry her if she chose to wait, and not be quite so "independent." Miss Mary wished she could acquit herself of all blame; a certain amount of limited novel reading had so imbued her mind with a horror of the mercenary marriages in the "high life" they spoke of, that she had determined Bertha never should become a victim, and she had done all she could in earlier days to prevent the possibility of such a catastrophe. Now she felt as if her anxiety on one hand had assisted to drive Bertha to the opposite extreme.

Mr. Francis Herbert, the hero of Bertha's romance, was a thoroughly good, conscientious, and well-meaning man, with an, unfortunately, abrupt and uningratiating manner. One of his great charms in Bertha's eyes was his straightforwardness. His was a singularly isolated position; an orphan from an early age, he had no home ties, no brother with whom the battles of childhood had been fought, no sister, to act as a refining influence. Bertha was frank, kind-hearted, liberal, and clever. Everything she chose to do she did well.

Full of self-confidence, she imagined that she had only to see a difficulty to overcome it.

Poverty! why, *she* would not miss her maid; had she not repeatedly dressed her own hair to her own and everybody else's satisfaction?

Carriages! except the fun of driving her spirited ponies, she preferred walking. Riding! why, that she might often indulge in, without keeping her own horse; and, besides, it was quite pleasant not to be chained down to these requirements, small sacrifices like these she surely could make. When, therefore, Mr. Herbert, after looking very ill indeed for some time, and making himself immensely disagreeable to everybody round him, confided to her the love, the devotion he had for her—his extreme wretchedness—spoke of his miserable prospects, and avowed the cause of his low spirits, Bertha, touched by finding herself the object of so much affection, consoled him, by avowing a very great regard for him, and finished by accepting him. "We shall be very, very poor," said Mr. Herbert. "I do not in the least mind that!" said Bertha; and so her fate was settled.

CHAPTER III.

MISS THURSTON REMONSTRATES WITHOUT EFFECT.

Lady Haughton congratulated Bertha so much more warmly than she had expected, and said so much in praise of Mr. Herbert's character, that Bertha felt as if she had never done her justice. The two people from whom she had expected the warmest congratulations were the two who disappointed her most.

Sir Luke looked grave and annoyed, and said just enough against the prudence of such a marriage to rouse Bertha's spirit of opposition. Had *she* to expect the fate of some of her literary heroine acquaintances, and stand up alone, and against her "cruel uncle," in favour of a pure and disinterested attachment? So she overwhelmed Sir Luke with such a voluble statement of her feelings, principles, and attachment, and justified her choice in such magniloquent English, that her kind uncle retreated before so much vehemence. It was very fatiguing; and Sir Luke yielded the point, and kissed his niece, if he did not congratulate her.

The person, however, from whom, above all others, Bertha expected sympathy and congratulation, was Miss Mary Thurston. How often had they not discussed together the wretchedness of mercenary marriages! How often had not Bertha, her eyes flashing with indignation over the recital of some impoverished lover left in the lurch by a worldly love, proclaimed that *she* would not take money, or position, or worldly advantages of any kind, into consideration when *she* thought of marrying! When, therefore, she dispatched a hasty note to

Miss Mary, summoning her to a cup of tea in her dressing-room at five o'clock, and added, "I have something very important to tell you"—with a great many dashes to prove, in language feminine, that it *was* very important indeed—she felt certain that Miss Mary would soon be embracing and congratulating her, with a happy but tearful face, as had often been the case on occasions of less moment, only the congratulations would be much more fervent, and the embraces a good deal warmer. As soon, however, as that excellent little woman made her appearance, and had arrived at a proper understanding of the reason of the blushing face and incoherent manner, Bertha was dismayed to see anxiety and disappointment in her countenance and sorrow in every gesture.

"Mr. Francis Herbert! My poor dear child!" was all she said, but the tone of voice was expressive enough. "Sir Luke —surely, he will never allow it?" she added, before Bertha's dismay had found vent in words, and putting the finishing stroke to her indignation.

"He will," said Bertha, in a tone of the deepest reproach. "Is this," she continued, "really your view of my marriage? *You*, from whom I expected the warmest sympathy? If I felt sure of one person in the world, that person was you! And now, forgetting how often this subject has been discussed between us—how often we have agreed together about it, you take this tone. What did you expect? Did you fancy *me* chained for life to some rich old man? Did you think *I* would marry for an establishment?"

"There is a wide difference, my dear Bertha, between marrying *for* money and marrying without it. By your account you will be poor. What is your idea of poverty?"

"Poverty," returned Bertha, "is comparative. Frank has three hundred a year, and I have four hundred; so we shall be able to have salt with our bread, if we can afford no other luxuries."

"Seven hundred a year would be wealth to some people, Bertha, but not to you. You literally know nothing about the management of money. You have no idea how little of what you now think necessaries you will be able to have with that income. Granted that you can manage quite at first. What will you do if you have a family to bring up—boys to educate —their professions——"

Bertha burst out laughing. "My dear little woman!" she exclaimed, "you really look too far forward. I feel quite an old woman already, with all the cares of a family upon my shoulders." And she shrugged those shoulders expressively.

"You may laugh, my dear," said Miss Mary, a little hurt at the failure of her remonstrances—"you may laugh; but I am right. As I said before, seven hundred a year would be an ample income to some people; many manage easily on less. But to you, with the habits of luxury you have, it will be poverty. Yes," continued poor Miss Mary, as sundry experiences of her own early days recurred to her memory, " nothing is—nothing can be so wretched as being obliged to maintain a position your fortune cannot support—the wearisome endless economies, the petty thrift!— it would be misery, absolute misery to you, Bertha; it *is* misery to any one with habits of refinement!"

Bertha was a little startled by her friend's eloquence, but she had far too much confidence in her own judgment to allow that she was wrong, or even that she had never weighed this side of the question; so she effectually turned the subject by rushing to the conservatory to produce a new " specimen," and consoled herself for her friend's want of sympathy—first, by reminding herself that Miss Mary was " an old maid," and not at all " in love;" secondly, that she had sometimes been in what might be called a croaking humour, in the old schoolroom days, and that she was evidently in a very croaking mood at present. Time would prove who was right.

CHAPTER IV.

LADY HAUGHTON THINKS SHE MUST INTERFERE.

Things went on at Haughton very much the same as usual. Bertha's nearest relations (two aunts and sundry cousins) were not sufficiently interested in her to care much about her marriage. During her father's lifetime Bertha had never cared about leaving home, and invitations at stated times were willingly declined by Sir Clement, who hated exertion in any shape; and the occasional "invasion" (as Bertha called the visits of these said relations) did not give peculiar pleasure to either party. Sir Clement's shooting was capital, and well preserved;

so the gentlemen enjoyed his coverts and praised his wine, while their wives disapproved of his establishment and abused his daughter.

To tell the truth, Bertha had not much chance of being popular with her relations, or any one else, till the angles of her character were rounded off by contact with the world. Unchecked by the motherly hand that can best restrain a temper like hers, and spoiled by her father (who thought everything she said and did was wonderfully clever), she had been accustomed to take the lead in the narrow circle round her, and had acquired a certain decision of manner and tone of independence that offended every one accustomed to the polished courtesy of good society. Her aunts called her "odd," and considered her "clever," but they gave her credit for conceit and an overbearing disposition—faults which were certainly not hers. She had been so much accustomed to her father's society, and to that of a few literary friends of his, who found Haughton a pleasant retreat now and then during his lifetime, that she had imbibed a strong prejudice in favour of men's society. The few women she knew occupied themselves generally by remarking upon the state of their own nurseries and those of their neighbours, abused or praised their servants, and picked holes in somebody's domestic arrangements. Bertha concluded all were alike; it was all weariness. So altogether she had escaped the friendships common to her sex, and was pronounced "eccentric"—a word that, like charity, covers a multitude of sins.

Now she was engaged to be married, Bertha was quite content to allow everything to remain as it was for the present. Her uncle said there was no hurry, and she quite agreed with him; but naturally enough, Mr. Herbert took a different view of the question, and he found a most unexpected ally in Lady Haughton.

Lady Haughton's calm selfishness had been a good deal disturbed lately. Mr. Herbert was sometimes there and sometimes not, which gave a little extra trouble. Then, according to her ideas, Bertha was very unsettled and extremely thoughtless; three times in one day, as her ladyship plaintively told Sir Luke, Bertha had rushed in at one door and out at another, like a kind of whirlwind, and left both doors open! "And, my dear, the draught was really terrible, though I was reading the third volume of 'Lady Helen's Crime,' and was trying to understand why some lady's husband was poisoned, and who somebody's wife really belonged to, and was dreadfully anxious about them all; and the deaths, and all that. I had to get up myself and shut the doors, and I dropped my book, and lost my place; and it was such a time before

I could find it again that I had quite forgotten the beginning before I got to the end. When are they to be married, Sir Luke?" continued her ladyship, finding scanty notice taken of her grievance.

"I really do not know, my dear," answered he; "there is no hurry."

"You always say there is no hurry," said Lady Haughton, peevishly. "It is all very well for you, with nothing to think about; but I have got so much to do, and it never does to hurry workpeople. They always charge more, and destroy the material, and blame you for having hurried them."

"What have you got to do, my dear?" inquired Sir Luke, whose opinion of his wife's powers of doing anything was very slight indeed.

"Why, all Bertha's things. I suppose I must see about all her things?"

"Things!" said Sir Luke; "what things?"

"Why, flannel petticoats and things," said Lady Haughton; "everybody has to get new things when they marry."

"I suppose you mean a trousseau?" said Sir Luke; "but I do not suppose it is necessary to begin to get that yet. They will be very poor," said he half to himself; "I do not like the idea of it at all."

Lady Haughton waxed impatient. "I do not see what they are to wait for!" she said, fretfully; "ten years hence they will not be any richer than they are now, and Bertha is quite old enough to know her own mind, and she always will have her own way. I remember the first time I tried to interfere about her dress— it was a green she would have, a pale green —I said all sorts of things to her about it; but she *would* have it; and it is just the same with everything else."

"Well, my dear," said Sir Luke, "nothing can be done till her uncle, Mr. Germayne, comes to England; *he* manages her money matters. If he comes home this month, Herbert can run up to London and see him; nothing need be done till then."

"Why do you want to put off this marriage?" said his wife, whose selfishness led her to read Sir Luke's feelings better than usual.

"Because, my dear, I think, by-and-by, I might be in a position to do something for them myself."

"With a family of your own!" said Lady Haughton, touched in her tenderest point; "it would *never* do." And rendered actually energetic by such a prospect her ladyship registered a little vow, and proceeded to try if Mr. Herbert could not be stirred up to better effect.

CHAPTER V.

LADY HAUGHTON TURNS DIPLOMATIST.

Between Lady Haughton and Mr. Francis Herbert there had always existed a calm and indifferent, but, on the whole, a friendly feeling.

Mr. Herbert knew that Lady Haughton considered this engagement a bore and a great trial of her patience, and he was not very much surprised when she began to speak to him in a tone of condolence; but as she proceeded, he, having no key to help him to understand her motives, felt surprised at the interest she evinced in his affairs, and like Bertha accused himself of having undervalued her.

"You are not looking well," began her ladyship, as she laid down on her lap the printed sorrows she was reading when he came into the room; "you really are not looking well, and" (with a little sigh) "no wonder; a long engagement is a very trying thing."

"The truth is, Lady Haughton, I do not understand what we are waiting for. We shall never be better off than we are now; and Bertha is old enough to judge for herself what her chances of happiness are with a limited income."

"Very true," said my lady, with another little sigh, "and just what I say to Sir Luke. The fact is," she continued, lowering her voice mysteriously, "that everything is waiting for Mr. Germayne; I found that out to-day."

"Mr. Germayne! Bertha's uncle?" inquired Mr. Herbert.

"Yes; Bertha's uncle by marriage."

"What has he got to do with it?" asked Mr. Herbert; "he is not her guardian, or anything of that sort."

"Oh dear, no!" answered Lady Haughton. "Bertha's father never left in his will that she was to have a guardian; but, somehow or other, I do not quite know how, Mr. Germayne has always managed Bertha's money matters, and he always pays her her money when she wants any. The fact is," continued Lady Haughton, "that when my dear Sir Luke came into this place, and all that, you know, he and this Mr. Germayne (who is most terribly plain, by the way, and not at all like a gentleman) had quite a quarrel about Bertha's money. Sir Luke said it was not well arranged in some way, *in*—something he called it—I remember——"

"Invested?" suggested Mr. Herbert.

"Yes; invested. Well, he, that is Sir Luke, wanted this money put, or invested, or something, on the property, or in the property—I do not quite understand all those complicated things about money—and Mr. Germayne said that it would be a great pity, and that Sir Luke had no right to interfere; and I remember Sir Luke saying it sounded all very well, but she had better have a certain sum every year than have more at one time and less at another."

Here Lady Haughton paused, exhausted by the efforts she had made to remember and say all she was now saying.

"So Mr. Germayne's absence is the cause of the delay?" said Mr. Herbert. "When is he expected, and where does he live generally?"

"In London. He is a great man for making long speeches in Parliament, and I sometimes look at them, in case he should come down here. I never understand the speeches; but," added her ladyship, candidly, "very likely that is because I only read the end, and look to see if there are a great many 'hears' throughout."

"And as Parliament meets next week,

I suppose he will be in London then," said Mr. Herbert.

" Of course he will," said Lady Haughton.

"Well," said Mr. Herbert, "I will go and see him. I am really very much obliged to you, Lady Haughton. Everything seems quite clear to me now." And in better spirits than he had been in for some time, Mr. Herbert went to find Bertha, leaving Lady Haughton covered with self-complacency, feeling certain that the ball she had set rolling would roll to some purpose in Frank Herbert's energetic hands.

CHAPTER VI.

IN WHICH SIR LUKE HAUGHTON'S CHARACTER IS DISCUSSED.

Sir Luke Haughton was a very popular man, with of course the "few exceptions" that prove the rule. He was handsome, beyond what is usually meant by that term —face and figure had an indescribable charm; gay, courteous, and kind-hearted, he was generous to a fault. In fact, he frequently gave what in justice was not his to give—a weak point in his character that Lady Haughton counteracted with all the energy of which her drowsy nature was capable.

He was not a vain man—that is, of his personal appearance; but he had his little weaknesses. Possessed of one of those frank, friendly natures, that are pliable as silk in skilful hands, he imagined himself a man of great determination, whose stronger will ruled all the minds around him. He believed that he exercised a great influence on all those with whom he came in contact, and plumed himself (in secret) on the supposed deference paid to his opinions.

He was the universal chairman of every local board, and was perpetually engaged in a petty warfare in defence of some action or expression, springing from some obscure question connected with county business. Agricultural shows, the decision of the judges, some new theory which he thought would revolutionize something, his active brain was ever at work; and his ready pen was only too frequently pressed into his service in defence of his opinions. Conscious of expressing himself well, he did not dislike to see his well-rounded periods in print, and the county newspaper often inserted letters from him—public grievances concerning society at large, or private wrongs relating to himself. It did not much matter what was the cause. Turnips!—the disrespect shown to the said turnips by some partial antagonist, the inferiority of the rival (and successful) esculents—away glided his pen to the battle. In language courteous but lofty he defended his vegetables, expending a great deal of energy, and some very good English, in the exposition of his feelings.

The only drawback connected with his county business was, that too frequently the meetings over which he presided (called with great ceremony and strict attention to the required rules) were attended only by himself, the clerk, and one or two juvenile members of the neighbouring families, who studied " county business," and tried Sir Luke's patience by systematically opposing every proposition that emanated from " the chair."

The county gentlemen generally were glad to have the business so well attended to, and eased their consciences by bestowing a little private ridicule on the industry they were not ambitious of imitating; they might ridicule him as they liked, Sir Luke was not only what is called a " clever" man, but he had a particular aptitude for business; and had he only bestowed as much thought and attention upon his private as he did upon his public business, things would have been different, and perhaps this story would never have been written.

As it was, the county newspaper held him up as an example to surrounding county gentlemen, printed his letters, and when news was scarce, and a letter valuable, did them full justice in the way of type. A letter would appear from Sir Luke; an answer, slightly abusive, would follow; " A Disinterested Bystander," or " Fair

Play" added a zest (both letters probably being editorial compositions), and the whole was quietly finished by the editor if he had anything better to put in. As a landlord, Sir Luke shone conspicuous; he was idolized by his tenantry, whom he never oppressed, and to whom, as to his equals, he showed that courteous gentleness of manner that is not to be learnt, for it is the natural expression of a gentleman at heart.

CHAPTER VII.

THE OTHER UNCLE.

It can readily be imagined that Bertha's marriage was not one that heartily pleased Sir Luke. If he had been in a position to come forward handsomely, and give her an increase of income, he would have reconciled himself to it with a much better grace. As it happened, Sir Luke was powerless. The estate was embarrassed when he succeeded to it, and of all men in the world he was the very last likely to put it right. Fond of his model farm, he detested the accounts connected with it; and when he did meet his bailiff his aptitude for business was displayed by summarily disposing of a mass of figures, with a celerity that inspired that honest man with a grave doubt as to how far his accounts were examined at all—doubts now and then set at rest in a very complete manner by the immediate detection of an error, probably in the pence line, which Sir Luke would rectify in a few minutes, and present to his astonished and admiring factotum with an excusable feeling of satisfaction.

Now that Francis Herbert had discovered the importance of Mr. Germayne's arrival, the parliamentary reports were no longer carefully scanned; his path was clear—he must wait upon that "other" uncle, and propitiate him. He found one day that Mr. Germayne must have arrived in London, as a short speech of his on some obscure question had elicited the "hear" for which Lady Haughton always looked, and was reported at length. He prepared, therefore, to depart, and consulted Sir Luke about his best mode of proceeding.

Sir Luke, who was very open, showed directly that Mr. Germayne was no favourite of his by the way in which he overwhelmed Frank with good advice about his first interview. "Be guarded, my dear Herbert," he said; "be guarded. Whatever you do, don't commit yourself to anything."

"Is Mr. Germayne very formidable?" asked Frank, who was amused at Sir Luke's counselling anything so unlike his own way of "getting on."

"Well, yes!—no, that is to say," said Sir Luke, fairly puzzled how to explain himself without prejudicing his hearer, "*we*, somehow, never hit it off together. Germayne's a very clever fellow, a deuced clever fellow, in fact; and when you think you have quite brought him round to your way of thinking, he surprises you by allowing you to find out he has got the better of you somehow. However, all you've got to do is to be guarded, and I dare say you'll get on with him very well." This was the amount of information Sir Luke chose to bestow; and Frank Herbert left Haughton with a feeling of dread for which he could not exactly account.

In a well-furnished, roomy house in Spring Gardens Mr. Germayne resided. He was a very useful member; and though he had avowedly nothing to do with Ministers, he was often a good deal more behind the scenes than most other county members.

His talents were very variously estimated; some of his friends looked upon him as a rising man, and others declared that his *one* talent lay in judicious silence and a look of great intelligence when some subject was brought forward of which he probably knew nothing. His ruling passion was ambition. Born to inherit a scanty patrimony, his earliest discovery was, that to succeed in the world you require one of three things—a great deal of money, a great deal of tact, or a great deal of talent. Of these three things he flattered himself he possessed the second to a degree that enabled him to do without either the first or third. He *was* clever to a certain extent—perhaps shrewd is more exactly the term for him—and he applied himself while yet quite a young man to the study of his fellow-men.

Of course there were some characters that completely baffled him; a man whose whole ideas were absorbed in self, and how self could be made to prosper, could not understand a thoroughly unselfish character, such, for instance, as Sir Luke Haughton. Self-contained, grave, and dignified, his very ugliness served him in good stead. No one had ever seen him laugh heartily, and his smile was a bitter one. When he spoke in a few low, measured words, he gave everyone an impression of having much in reserve; and after carefully watching himself in his more youthful days, the grave, saddened gaze that met yours was in time habitual to him.

By degrees he gathered things around him; one "little thing" and another was presented to him by friends in power impressed with a sense of his merits, and at forty he held an enviable position. Nominally poor, he was really rich, and was one of those from whom nothing was ever expected, and yet who really had plenty to give.

Mr. Germayne showed to particular advantage in his study. The stained-glass windows, with their crimson draperies; the old oak cabinets, black with age and looking like mysteries; the carved high-backed chair in which he sat; and the study table, littered with rolls of paper, parchments, plans, manuscripts, and letters—all was in keeping with the stern, square face of the proprietor. Impossible not to be impressed with a picture when every detail was in such good keeping.

Frank Herbert was so much impressed when he was ushered into the presence of his future uncle, that it was with a great feeling of intrusion that he advanced and begged for a few minutes of Mr. Germayne's valuable time.

Mr. Germayne half rose, bowed, and sat down again, waving Frank into a seat close to him, and moving aside various papers which, to the young man's inexperienced eyes, looked like a sort of chaos.

"I am very glad to see you, Mr. Herbert," he said, in slow and melodious accents. "I have written till I feel quite tired" (glancing at a heap of letters lying ready for the post beside him) "and a little conversation will refresh me."

"I suppose you know all about me?" said Frank, whose small stock of self-possession vanished completely under the cool calm gaze of his auditor.

"I cannot go so far as to say that," answered Mr. Germayne; "it is a question if all about any one ever is known."

"I meant about my engagement to your niece, Miss Haughton," said Frank.

"Yes," Mr. Germayne said, with his pleasant voice and disagreeable smile; "Sir Luke Haughton's letter, some months ago, told me of your proposal, and of its acceptance; but these affairs *sometimes go off.* The engagement still exists?"

"Yes," said Frank, who felt considerably irritated on hearing his engagement and their affection laid open to the suspicion of change; "I came to see you about it."

"Me!" said Mr. Germayne, looking inquiringly at Frank's face.

"I want to know exactly all about Bertha's money matters," said straightforward Frank, who had now roused himself into action.

Mr. Germayne smiled. "What are your own prospects?" he asked.

Frank's brow grew hot. "I have exactly three hundred a year," he said, feeling, for the first time in his life, how absurdly small such a provision was.

Mr. Germayne started. "Three—hundred—a year!" he repeated, "and expectations?"

"None."

Nothing could have reduced poor Frank to such a feeling of being "shut up" as the expressive silence that followed.

"Bertha had nominally ten thousand pounds," said Mr. Germayne, "when her father died."

"Nominally?" Frank repeated.

"Yes, nominally—that is to say, Sir Clement left her that sum; but when he died the estate was so very much embarrassed that it was not his to leave. It was never completely realized."

Frank bowed, as Mr. Germayne paused for an expression of some kind from him.

"I felt very much for Bertha Haughton, Mr. Herbert," continued Mr. Germayne—"*very* much, though she is no blood relation (being, as you are aware, my deceased wife's niece); and I had (being supposed to have some little knowledge of business) been frequently consulted about her father's affairs. I therefore took upon me the management of her little fortune. Now, Mr. Herbert, there are certain circumstances connected with her affairs that—I will not trouble you with needless details; indeed, if I did, I don't think you could possibly understand them."

Frank felt mystified. "You think I could not understand them?" he asked.

"I am certain of it; your mind is not trained to business—details would simply puzzle you. I daresay you think this very absurd; but it is not so. How often——" Here Mr. Germayne paused, as if lost in thought. Suddenly leaning forward, he said, impressively, "I am going to place great confidence in you, Mr. Herbert—a foolish confidence, some might think, on so slight an acquaintance. *I do not think it foolish.*" Frank felt pleased, and showed it. " When I looked into Sir Clement's affairs I found that he had directed this sum of money (Bertha's fortune) to be invested on realization in a certain way. Mr. Herbert, the portion of it that was realized I did not so invest. No," continued Mr. Germayne, "I ran the risk of being misunderstood; and I acted as I felt was best for Bertha's interest. Sir Clement, in a memorandum that he left, begged that I would act for her; and though it was vaguely expressed, and gave me no legal powers, yet I acted for the best. Now, in telling you all this, Mr. Herbert, I am placing myself, to a certain degree, in your power. There are many who would hesitate to do so: I do not hesitate."

"I assure you," said Frank, warmly, and completely carried away by the influence of the man before him, " no confidence can ever be more safe. I shall hold it sacred."

"I am sure of it," said Mr. Germayne. "Now, I am going to be perfectly frank with you. I have told you that I took upon myself, for Bertha's good, to disregard the wishes expressed in Sir Clement's will (or rather memorandum), and I invested Bertha's money in a different way; in so doing I at once doubled her income. Now," he continued, preventing Frank's reply by a gesture of his hands, "in strict confidence I must tell you this: if, in consequence of Bertha's marriage and the necessary settlements, your lawyer examines into all this — it is just possible he may, seeing with the eyes of the law and not of relationship—he may advise— yes, that's the word — he may advise Bertha's money being placed on a different footing. She, it is true, would lose nearly half her income; but your professional man does not think about that. He will think more of his law and less of her."

"But," interrupted Frank, "if Mr. Carter (who is my man of business), if he advises anything so decidedly contrary to our interest, there is no reason in the world why we should follow his advice."

"Certainly not," said Mr. Germayne; "but you forget that I should perhaps be placed in a very uncomfortable position. I should be forfeiting my character as a strict man of business if it were generally known that I had been governed by my feelings in this way. Add to this," he continued, "that, out of consideration to others, I should not feel justified in allowing Mr. Carter, or any one else, to examine all *my* private affairs."

Mr. Herbert's countenance fell. "I do not see what is to be done," said he, despondingly, and trying to understand the difficulty.

"Wait," said Mr. Germayne.

"We have already waited so long," said Frank Herbert, whose spirits fell considerably on the receipt of this advice.

"It is quite possible that in another year or so I may be in a position to come forward openly about Bertha's money, and allow Mr. Carter or any one else to see all my private papers," said Mr. Germayne.

"I cannot see," said poor Mr. Herbert, "why any change should be made. Why cannot the money continue to be paid to Bertha just as it is now, without any fuss? And Mr. Carter—he is a very good man, and very kind, and all that; but cannot we do without him?"

"I should say yes, decidedly," said Mr. Germayne; "but then I am on the wrong side of the house. The fact is simply this, my dear Mr. Herbert: it rests with yourself, or rather I should say you and Bertha; two courses lie open to you—either put off your marriage for a year or so (a course, I must say, I strongly advise), when Mr. Carter, or any other lawyer, is welcome to see everything connected with Bertha's fortune; or allow my man of business, Mr. Flipson, to act for you, thus bringing no stranger into our counsels."

"Surely," exclaimed Mr. Herbert, hope springing up again as a possible outlet to their difficulties appeared; "there can be no possible objection to that. I suppose all lawyers are alike: one can make a settlement for us as well as another."

"The world," smiled Mr. Germayne, "thinks differently. When two young people are going to be married, their two respective family lawyers meet, and each endeavours to make the best bargain he can for his client—so much pin-money, such an allowance in case of premature demise. In a gentleman-like way, each drives the best bargain he can."

"But in *our* case it is quite different," said Mr. Herbert. " Whom does all this arrangement rest with ?"

" With yourself, as your father is no longer living."

" Then everything is easily settled," said Mr. Herbert. " Well, I do see my way now, I think."

" If you think you are able to look after your own interests," said Mr. Germayne, " you can see Flipson to-morrow; and here is his address. When he reports progress I shall send Sir Luke a little note about it all. I shall, of course, shape my course a little by yours. I am sorry to seem inhospitable, but I have a mass of work to get through. Good-bye. I am glad we so thoroughly understand each other." With his most candid expression he shook hands with his nephew-elect, the bell was rung, an old man with silvery hair and majestic gait ushered Frank to the front door, and that part of the play was played out.

" Understand each other! Do we?" thought Frank, as the fresh air revived his bewildered intellects; "I have no doubt he understands me and himself too, but I'll be hanged if I understand him. He is the most puzzling old fellow to talk to I ever met. He talks as if Bertha ought to be grateful, or I ought to be grateful, about something he could not exactly explain, and which would compromise everybody if I understood. I feel like a Lord Dundreary at this moment. However, somehow, the difficulty—whatever it is—is so far over. I'll see this Mr. Flipson the first thing tomorrow, and go and write Bertha a full account of the interview at once."

CHAPTER VIII.

MATRIMONIAL.

When Frank Herbert's letter reached Haughton, Bertha (omitting the adjectives) read so much of it to Sir Luke as enabled him to feel afraid that Frank had been "committing" himself. Mr. Flipson, he thought and said, was a rascal; but as Bertha had grown accustomed to hear Mr. Flipson stigmatized as a rascal, it created in her mind no feeling of distrust. Her dealings with him were very simple: she wrote to enclose Madame So-and-so's little account, or heard from him that Madame Telle-et-telle had sent one in. In the first case she would receive a few lines from him to say that it had been or would be attended to; in the second, she wrote to request he would attend to it. She knew Sir Luke disliked Mr. Germayne; but with that self-confidence which formed so great a part of her character, she set down Sir Luke's feelings, not to the honest distrust of an upright character, instinctively disliking something shuffling and anything *but* upright, but to a want of sympathy, caused by the different lives they led and the different directions in which their talents found vent. Bertha, completely misled by Mr. Germayne's reticence and gravity, looked upon him as an intellectual giant, while Sir Luke lost in her estimation by comparison, and she always thought, "If Sir Luke had been clever he never would have married Lady Haughton;" by which it will be seen that she did not consider Lady Haughton in the light of an intellectual giant; it also proves that her knowledge of the world was limited.

Sir Luke wrote to Frank, beginning his

letter with an earnest hope that he had not "committed" himself, and giving Frank so capital an outline of the supposed interview between him and Mr. Germayne, that Frank was fairly convulsed with laughter. Sir Luke, however, went on, in all seriousness, to entreat Frank to consult Mr. Carter, or one or two other men, whose addresses he sent, before he finally settled anything. His warning was so solemn that it could not but be accepted by Frank, who, however, felt that he was not in a position to do anything of the kind. How could he drag Mr. Carter or any other lawyer into Mr. Germayne's confidence after what had passed? He called on Mr. Germayne, who was never "at home;" then he wrote to him: he was answered in a few lines. Sir Luke was disposed of in a few words. It was hinted, kindly, but as if forbearingly, that Sir Luke was well intentioned, but a better judge of sheep than he could be of law. It was the old story—the crooked mind surrounded the straight one, and, for the time, obscured it.

Under these circumstances the result was natural enough: Sir Luke's letters, even one from Mr. Carter, produced no effect; one or two more interviews with Mr. Flipson put everything to rights. Frank was immensely complimented by that gentleman on his extensive knowledge of business (!) till he thought perhaps he might have an undeveloped talent in that way, lying dormant for want of practice; and Mr. Germayne sent a fair and flourishing letter to Sir Luke, giving him an outline of the settlements. *All Bertha's fortune* was strictly settled upon herself and possible family, and these preliminaries settled, Frank sold out of the army, things in general prospered, and at length the marriage took place, and the bells which struck so discordant a tone on Miss Priscilla's ears announced the fact to all within hearing.

CHAPTER IX.

MUNDANE MATTERS.

SOME few months passed away. Bertha and Frank did what most other people do: they peeped into foreign churches (old friends of Bertha's girlhood), floated up (or down) the Rhine, climbed up hills, and made themselves thoroughly uncomfortable for a fixed period; and then, having done their duty, they returned to England.

Not far from London they proposed taking up their residence, and took lodgings (that they might look about them) in a pretty country town on the Great Northern Railway.

Bertha's first view of her married life was, that she could afford *nothing!*

With this exaggerated idea of the smallness of their income, she felt it right to be strictly economical. She doled out the tea in starved tea-spoonfuls, grudged herself sugar, and felt it "right" to go herself to the butcher's. Her first visit there is worth recording. In her most dignified manner (hating the smell of the shop as much as the sight of the meat), she asked for "something for dinner," not specifying anything in particular, and by her whole demeanour much puzzling the individual whose ample form was shrouded in a blue linen apron. Judging from her appearance that it was a case of a very large order, the butcher advanced towards her cheerfully, brandishing, at the same time, his well-sharpened knife.

"Certainly, 'm; for use to-day?"

"Yes; for to-day," answered Bertha.

"Well, 'm, there's a great choice. Roast —every joint in *prime* order. *Excellent* boiling pieces; *leg* of mutton, *fore*-quarter of lamb, *loin* of mutton, leg of *weal* (excellent fillet that leg would make). What shall I have the pleasure of sending you, 'm?"

His rapidity of utterance took away Bertha's courage; he seemed so perfectly prepared to send her the whole contents of his shop on the faintest encouragement, and all the joints looked *so* large.

Despair at last drove her to say, "Will you be so good as to show me how large a piece of meat I can buy for sixpence?"

The butcher's countenance was a perfect study; astonishment, incredulity, and bewilderment succeeded each other, giving place finally to a look of compassion, as he silently placed about half a pound of beefsteak before his customer.

"Three times that quantity will do," said Bertha, utterly unconscious of having raised any extraordinary emotions in the mind of so ordinary an individual, and much relieved on finding it so easy to get exactly what she wanted; hastily paying for it, and leaving her address, she relieved the butcher by disappearing.

It must be confessed that the dinner looked small that day. In the hands of a good French cook what numberless little dishes could have been produced from the same materials! But in the hands of an unmitigated English cook, of a decidedly inferior sort, it appeared not exactly in a tempting guise—hard, greasy, dried up, as to the meat, and flavourless as to the gravy. Frank was not long enough "head of the family" as yet to say much, and, besides, he was immensely amused by his wife's account of her marketing. He suggested a little consultation with Mrs. Jones, their landlady, and Bertha was only too glad to avail herself of Mrs. Jones's experience. But still, she always had an uncomfortable conviction that they might be exceeding their income; and when the end of the month came and she made up her accounts, she was astonished and delighted with the result: forgetting that except a trifling purchase, such as a skein of silk, &c., she had not been obliged to get a single thing in the shape of clothing for herself or her husband—that it was summer, consequently no firing and comparatively little light had been used. She took her accounts to her husband, who, with herself, was perfectly charmed, and they exulted over it together.

"Why, at this rate, we shall save a great quantity of money every year," said Frank, scanning over the various items, written in Bertha's firmest and most distinct handwriting.

"Yes," answered his wife; "and, of course, I see little mistakes here that I shall take care to avoid another time. One learns so much experience in this practical sort of way."

"It just shows," said Frank, "what utter nonsense people talk about incomes—trash!"

"Does it not?" said his wife. "*Who* said I should be a bad poor man's wife? We have been *very* happy, and we have spent so *very* little!"

CHAPTER X.

FRANK HERBERT BUYS EXPENSIVE THINGS, STRICTLY ON PHILOSOPHICAL PRINCIPLES.

At some little distance from the modest lodging of Mrs. Jones there was a pretty cottage, in a picturesque and healthy situation, standing in the centre of its own grounds, which comprised about five acres, chiefly occupied by ornamental trees. It was unfurnished; but this the Herberts thought was a great recommendation.

"So much wiser," Herbert said, "to buy nice, useful, sensible furniture, than to have to pay a great deal for great, heavy, ricketty things. I remember once, when my poor mother was alive, we had a furnished house at Weymouth, and not a table stood steady;

the chairs were all weak, and went to pieces when you touched them. The people made us pay enormously for things we knew must have been cracked when we went into the house, and everything was *hideous.*"

Bertha was quite sure he must be right; so they took the cottage for a term of years.

It was a source of great amusement to them both, furnishing this house, and choosing all the carpets, curtains, &c., &c. Unluckily, they both had a very keen sense of what was in " good taste."

" I think it unwise," said Herbert, with the air of a philosopher, " to be rigid about a few shillings more or less where prettiness is concerned; nothing affects the spirits more than having ugly things about one."

On this principle they acted; no one could deny that the effect was beautiful, but the bills were large. They mounted their establishment on the most modest scale; and the only thing in the shape of mankind they engaged was a boy, or rather lad, of sixteen or seventeen years of age.

Mr. Herbert suffered (for a man of his temperament) little short of martyrdom under the influence of this " boy." In the first place, his boots were always badly cleaned, his clothes were never properly brushed or properly folded, and the constant skirmishes that went on exhibited her husband in quite a new light to Bertha.

" How you do scold that wretched Robert," said she one day; " why not discharge him and get another in his place? There are a great many boys in the world, and he seems very unsatisfactory."

" Another might be worse," rejoined her husband; " Robert is perfectly honest."

Bertha was sensible enough not to *say* that she thought, if a change was not desirable, such perpetual scoldings were a mistake; and her husband went on.

" Just look at the plate, though! I declare it is really *too* bad!" and he rose from his chair with an air of the greatest annoyance, and held out a large silver fork towards his wife.

Bertha took it dutifully, and turned it over and over. She was half ashamed to ask what was the matter with it. "It is certainly not very bright," she said, at length.

"Bright!" exclaimed her husband; "that's *nothing!* Why, it's scratched all over! And those spoons are *shamefully* cleaned!"

"They certainly do not look very nice," agreed Bertha; "but you cannot expect the duties of a first-rate servant from poor Robert."

"And, in the meantime, everything we possess is to be utterly ruined," said Mr. Herbert. "I declare it would be far better economy to get a really good servant at once than to lose all one's possessions in this unsatisfactory way. I have often heard what false economy it is to have cheap and inefficient servants, and now I can quite believe it."

In the meantime Bertha's troubles had well begun downstairs. The cook she had engaged was one with a flaming character; her virtues had been so enlarged upon, that Bertha could not understand why her periods of service had been invariably short. She was, to tell the truth, a good deal afraid of the bold, black-eyed woman, who presented herself on arrival in an immense hoop, hardly a bit of cap on her head, and a decision of manner that made Bertha feel it would be difficult to "find fault."

The day after their first interview, Bertha was feeling both ill and out of spirits, and after saying, with assumed firmness, that she trusted everything would be conducted with economy, &c., she dismissed her, considerably daunted by the steady gaze directed towards her by " the treasure."

No one knew but poor Bertha herself the troubles and trials of her first establishment; the servants found out immediately that she had not got one bit of useful experience, and took advantage of her in every possible way. They entertained their friends, went out at all hours, and played into each other's hands so as completely to set her at defiance. About their work it was exactly the same thing. Bertha had no idea whose duty it was to undertake certain parts of the household work, and therefore never could find fault with confidence. She had a sense of responsibility, and tried to look after them, but it was no earthly use, and Bertha felt sadly enough that her ideas of the relations between mistress and servant were Utopian, and acknowledged to herself that *here* she was defeated.

CHAPTER XI.

BREAKERS AHEAD!

THE post arrived at breakfast-time, and though Bertha's correspondence was of a limited and wholly uninteresting order, she shared in that general feeling of pleasurable expectation of hearing "news," which distinguishes those who have no experience of the unpleasant side of life. One morning, as frequently happened, having no letters of her own, she watched her husband peruse his letters, trying to discover if there was anything more interesting than usual by the expression of his countenance; she was surprised to see a look of great annoyance cross his features, and in answer to her anxious inquiries, he threw the letter across the table to her that had just been occupying him.

It was a letter from Mr. Flipson, merely saying that owing to circumstances (how Frank detested that word!) he would feel obliged if Mr. Herbert would forward him the amount of his account for professional advice, &c.; in short, it was the lawyer's bill for settlements, &c., which Mr. Germayne had intimated was to be *his* little present to Bertha, as Mr. Flipson was his own "man of business."

It was divided, as only lawyers know how, into sundry "items," and amounted altogether to the sum of one hundred and thirty-four pounds fifteen shillings and eightpence, one item being fifteen pounds fifteen shillings to a man whom Flipson introduced to Herbert under the pretext of not liking to have "the whole responsibility of advising," and who had passed about ten minutes in exalting and admiring Mr. Flipson's handiwork.

"There is some mistake," said Bertha, cheerfully, going to her husband's side as she spoke.

"It is of course some mistake," said he, but not quite so cheerfully; he remembered inconveniently at that moment, that Bertha's quarter's money had now been due some days, and he felt a little uncomfortable. "You had better write at once, dear, to Flipson, and remind him that the day of your payment is overdue, and I will enclose a note referring him for payment to your uncle, Mr. Germayne."

"I had better write to Uncle Germayne too," said Bertha; "he will be very angry with Flipson for making such a mistake."

Her husband assented, but could not shake off an uncomfortable conviction that something was wrong.

Bertha wrote to Mr. Flipson, forwarding at the same time a letter to Mr. Germayne. An answer addressed to her husband arrived from the agent by return of post.

He wrote coolly, and as if stating the most matter-of-fact event possible, premising, " That as ladies proverbially knew nothing of business he answered Mrs. Herbert's letter to her husband—that Mr. Germayne (whose affairs, he regretted to say, were in some confusion), had left for a prolonged tour in the East *viâ* Paris; and that before starting he had told him to send in his account to Mr. Herbert, who would see that it was paid; in conclusion, he begged to add, that not wishing to annoy Mrs. Herbert at the first outset of her marriage, he had (at some slight inconvenience) paid several accounts out of his own private funds, for which he would be glad to receive a cheque at her earliest convenience."

Bertha could not understand it. " What does he mean?" she cried, full of indignation; " he talks as if I had no money of my own; why does he not pay all these bills as usual?" Reading nothing but blank dismay in her husband's countenance she sank back in her chair, and gave way to a hearty fit of crying.

Irritated and annoyed as Frank was, he could not see his wife's first tears without emotion; and he tried to assume a cheerfulness, and assert a confidence in "all being right eventually," that he was very far from feeling, and soothed his wife by every argument he could think of. They both agreed that a letter must be sent to Sir Luke, and also one to Mr. Flipson, calling upon the former for advice and for explanation from the latter.

Soon, very soon, came Sir Luke's letter, *he* wrote angrily about Mr. Germayne, and furiously about Mr. Flipson; he was evidently grieved and distressed, all the more so that things had come to a climax with him. Haughton must be let, (Bertha thought degradation could go no farther!) and poor Sir Luke was to fret away his jovial English spirit for some years at an obscure French watering-place! It was evident that his life was so bitter to him at the present moment, that he could hardly compassionate any one—not condemned also to exile themselves.

"I always told you that Flipson was a rascal," wrote Sir Luke; "and now you find I'm right. I am very sorry you are having trouble so early in the day. I don't suppose," continued the kind-hearted man, "that Germayne will do such a scoundrelly thing as leave this payment on your hands; but still I don't like the tone of Flipson's letter. I suppose you will not take my advice (nobody does take advice till it's too *late* to do any good); but *I* should sent for Carter if I were you, and put myself in his hands at once; if I had it in my power I would go to you and see what could be done, but at this moment I am fairly worried upon every side. All my tenants have been failing, and Germayne's plans and investments are all failures also."

All his letter was written in a tone unlike himself; it was evident that Sir Luke, like Mr. Herbert, felt that something was wrong.

Frank Herbert felt bound in honour to Mr. Germayne, after what had passed between them, not to call upon Mr. Carter for assistance until he had tried what he could do by a personal application to him. He wrote again to Mr. Flipson, and enclosed a letter to Mr. Germayne.

This letter simply stated that he had allowed Mr. Flipson to arrange matters for him, on the distinct understanding that Mr. Germayne would charge himself with the expense; and supposing that Mr. Flipson had misunderstood the instructions forwarded to him. He also said that Bertha's yearly income was considerably over due, &c. &c.

In due course of time Mr. Flipson forwarded a letter received by him from Mr. Germayne:—

"My dear Sir,—I think, in regard to the notes you speak of, that Mr. B——d acted badly; but I never expect gratitude from any one, so I confess I am sorry, but not disappointed.

"The little railway bill in which B—— and I are interested, I think I shall be quite able to carry through next session. You may say so; do not speak of it as a *certainty*, but give them good grounds for hope.

"I am more grieved than I can say at those investments turning out so badly. I do not mind candidly owning to you that it is a matter of serious personal inconvenience to me at this moment, and I am vexed, as, from what you say, Mr. and Mrs. Herbert have already got into money difficulties. Alas! my niece, Mrs. Herbert, was the last person in the world who ought to have married a poor man. As long as I was able I was glad to pay her a fabulous interest for the money (which, though never realized, she was supposed to have), and should gladly have assisted them now, but as you know, my means are limited. I had intended making them a little present, in the shape of your professional services; but, alas! I am not in the position to do so. Let us hope that brighter days are in store for us all!

"Yours,
"E. GERMAYNE."

With a very pale face, Frank Herbert handed this letter to his wife, and left the room. He must be alone, to face the frightful possibilities that crowded upon him.

Bertha took the letter with a trembling hand, and endeavoured to understand all its significance. At this inopportune moment a large box was announced, which she hastily ordered to her room, and she retreated there, letter in hand. Mechanically she gazed at the contents displayed, when the officious maid had opened the lid and obeyed Bertha's orders "to leave her." The box contained some baby clothes; for Bertha expected soon to be a mother.

As in a dream, poor Bertha handled the dainty caps and robes so delicately made, and found herself wondering, not if *she* would live to see a sweet baby face in those caps—not thrilling all over with the sweet motherly feeling—but trying to remember what they cost, and how much her order came to! How she had looked forward to baby's *trousseau*, and longed to realize her hopes a little by handling all the dainty garments! Now their first sight brought her no pleasure; she remembered only that they had to be paid for!

CHAPTER XII.

FRANK HERBERT TRIES TO SEE HIS WAY.

WHILE Bertha, with a dull sense of pain, was making herself wretched upstairs—without exactly saying to herself what was wrong—Frank was walking along the road at his utmost speed, trying to calm himself by violent exercise, after the fashion of some excitable men.

His wife was, therefore, at this moment the most to be pitied of the two.

She was trying to recollect all that ever passed between her and Mr. Germayne about money matters, in his repeated confidential communications. All was vague; she remembered, always thanking him, because he always showed he expected to be thanked; but she could not put into shape a single thing. She tried to comfort herself now by dwelling upon his words, but she could not recollect one sentence in which anything certain had been said. Always a supposed kindness, always a little tone of mystery, a superiority *implied*, a sense of benefit impressed upon her—a supposed kindness and obligation insinuated. Nothing but this.

When, however, Bertha had been miserable for some time, the reaction of a sanguine and buoyant nature turned in her favour. After all, she thought, the money is mine, so Mr. Flipson's impertinence cannot affect us *really*, though it is very disagreeable and may bother us just now; but supposing that we have to spend some of our capital in paying off everything? Why we should still have plenty of money left. She blamed herself for having been so easily dismayed; it was all Frank's fault, and she must not allow herself to be carried away by his depressed views—in short, by that womanly way of arguing, Bertha fairly put herself into good spirits, much to the astonishment of her husband, who returned from a long walk and no luncheon, neither more cheerful nor more sanguine than he had been in the morning.

It is certainly a mortifying fact, how much our views of life are affected by our state of appetite, and the way the digestive organs have been treated. When Frank had dined (his dinner being all it ought to have been), his idea of their position improved very considerably. He bore with more patience Bertha's views of everything, and wrote a letter to Mr. Germayne, which was a very different production to the one which would have reached that gentleman had it been written a few hours sooner.

It began by saying that Mr. Germayne's letter to Mr. Flipson had been forwarded to him, and that its contents had astonished him very much, indeed so much, and so completely was he unable to understand it, that he had come to the conclusion that he understood nothing of business, and therefore had determined to call upon Mr. Carter, to see Mr. Flipson, and endeavour to arrive at some correct understanding as to their position, a step he had been urged to take some months previously, but had not done, as Mr. Germayne might recollect, at his express request. He now conceived that Mr. Germayne's letter (in which he regretted his inability to fulfil his engagement) released him from the tacit engagement he had rashly made not to bring a stranger into their counsels, &c. &c.

Mr. Germayne wrote a reply immediately, not to Mr. Herbert, but to his wife. Assuming throughout his letter a tone of wounded susceptibility, he reproached Bertha for allowing her husband to address him as he had done. "Amidst the turmoil and wear and tear of public life," he wrote, "his own gratification had been that he had always been able to pay her such a large sum yearly hitherto; it was entirely optional, and rested only on himself and his high sense of honour, for that he had not one shadow of legal obligation. It was too much that on a reverse of fortune *he* should be called upon as a responsible person; that the tone Mr. Herbert assumed put an end for ever to any further amicable arrangements or relations between them; that he now regretted *deeply* that he had ever been led to sanction her marriage to one who, having no profession, would, he was afraid, never do much for himself or improve her position; but she must remember he had urged them to wait, and she had only herself to blame. He urged the necessity of strict economy, and wound up with an exhortation to make the best of her position, and to trust, as he did, to a brighter day."

It was perfectly incomprehensible to Frank that his wife, after receiving this letter, should still look at things cheerfully; but the truth is, that to a woman brought up as Bertha had been, knowing nothing of the actual want of money, and nothing of the actual dishonesty want of money sometimes drags people into (who are utterly unscrupulous) the broad fact was this: the money was hers, and therefore, of course, she must have it in time. The idea of anything wrong, of her money being appropriated by her own relation, never for a moment suggested itself to her; and she thought to herself that it was Frank's own temperament that made him look so wretched, and take such terribly gloomy views of that miserable thing—money! So she tried her utmost to make him cheerful, and was constantly astonished at her want of success, and at the look of anxiety and care that for ever clouded his face.

CHAPTER XIII.

TROUBLED WATERS.

Nothing could have been a greater test of affection than the present position of the Herberts' affairs.

Frank, having written to Mr. Carter, and requested him to see Mr. Flipson and come to an understanding about things, fancied, after the fashion of some men, that it would do no good worrying his wife by constantly discussing their position, and kept feelings and thoughts to himself that would have been infinitely more bearable if aired by exposure to Bertha's fresh views of everything, and her sympathy.

It was doing her an injustice in every way, though a very unconscious one. Hers was essentially a nature that would improve by being subjected to some of the roughnesses of life; and brooding over the sorrows and the probabilities and possibilities that crowded upon him was peculiarly unwholesome for him, and affected his outward bearing very uncomfortably.

Far better if he had acted otherwise—far better if he had told her his worst fears, and lessened his anxieties by dividing them. How was Bertha to imagine that her husband's excessively cross answer to some trivial inquiry, was, in reality, not a special rebuke to her for having bored him with so trifling a matter, but paragraph No. 4 or 5 of Mr. Germayne's letter, which he had been brooding over till it assumed the most frightful and gigantic proportions.

Under even the most favourable circumstances Frank's position was a very trying one. Without a profession, without the duties of property, without any fixed occupation, not particularly given to literature, it may be imagined his time hung heavily enough upon his hands.

Bertha was not strong enough to be his constant companion out of doors, and she was too wise to bring her domestic troubles to her husband. She dreaded for him the fate that has befallen some idle men, and was conscious of the "confusion worse confounded" that is wrought when the head of the house—beginning, perhaps, by an honest and kind endeavour to help his wife out of her difficulties—imagines he has discovered in himself a peculiar aptitude for domestic management, and insists upon bringing to bear upon the unhappy household a spirit of inquiry—conducive, doubtless, to magnificent results when applied to mechanics, chemistry, or science in any shape—but fatal when used to drag to light the puerile and petty details of home economy.

No; Bertha kept her grievances of this sort to herself, if she had occasionally to smooth the cook into good humour, or to give up a scheme she intended as an improvement. She was both sensible and kind enough to feel that, in a very small household, it is one especial trial, and that the *genius* of housekeeping really consists in knowing what faults to pass over and what allowances to make. Impossible to expect from servants what you yourself, with all the advantages of education, &c. &c. *ad lib.*, could not give—perpetual good temper, perpetual activity, and perpetual carefulness.

She certainly had never had a very good opinion of her cook, and was not at all sorry to find that her husband considered her too expensive a servant for them in the doubtful position of their affairs; so, instead of confining her directions to the dinner and its component parts, she told her she wished to part with her, but that she would speak to her about it in the evening—it was for no special fault.

As the evening went on, Bertha, remembering the interview and explanation she had somewhat unwisely deferred in the morning, began to dread it immensely.

After thinking it over a little while, she retreated to bed, and put out all but one candle; and thus housed she felt her courage revive, and felt equal to confronting many cooks; so she summoned her to her room.

In the meantime, the female Soyer's day had not on the whole been a cheerful one. She was conscious of such a number of delinquencies that she spent her time in trying to find out which particular thing had been "found out." Was it the being "out," or was it her little arrangement about the suet? After all, she felt she could easily talk Mrs. Herbert over. "Missus" was far too inexperienced to be able to find fault with confidence; and so, when the summons came, she obeyed it without any fears as to her not having the best of it.

When, however, Bertha, in a clear voice, and a calm and perfectly unexceptionable manner, gave her to understand that she wished to part with her, and was beginning to speak of " those little things" that had so aggrieved her—the cook, dreading to find herself placed in the wrong, and spoken to in that very calm voice about things she could *not* defend, took the initiative at once.

" I onderstand, 'm, that you wish to part with me, 'm. Now, 'm, if there's ony think you particularly wish to say, 'm, I do beg in you'll say it an once, as I feel your situation most oncomfortable, and quite onlike onythink I've held since I've been cook. I've been quite disappointed, 'm—quite disappointed. Yours is a very poor place, 'm—a very poor place indeed. I thought when I came, being told you was daughter of one Barron Night, and niece of another Barron Night, it would be a very different thing. The parquisites, 'm, is nothing; you've never no dinners worth thinking about, and I lost my cooking most dreadful since I've come to you. I've not had no chance of keeping my hand in; so, if you please, 'm, I should like to leave at once—as soon as ever it's convenient."

"To-morrow," said Bertha. "I have had so much cause for dissatisfaction, putting aside your impertinence just now; that about character——"

"Oh, 'm, as to character, it wouldn't serve *me* much saying as I lived cook with you. When families keeps no company and gives no dinners, and is always taken up with economy ways——. Yours is a poor place, 'm—*a very poor place indeed.* Good evening, 'm." And before Bertha could recover from her surprise, and put in a single word, the woman, who had run this off with the most insolent air imaginable, bounced out of the room.

It is all very well talking about being superior to those sort of trials, and being above fretting over unmerited impertinence, but for the first time in her life Bertha had been subjected to insolence from a vulgar woman, and she was quite a person to feel it keenly. It might have afforded infinite satisfaction to the cook had she been able to see the bitter tears wrung from the chafed spirit of her mistress.

Wisely, however, Bertha neither curtailed nor enlarged upon this scene to Frank. She merely told him that the cook had been impertinent, and left him, if he pleased, to conjecture what had passed. Nothing he might imagine would exceed the truth.

CHAPTER XIV.

THE FRIENDLY LAWYER.

Not very long after all this, and before Bertha had been able to replace the invaluable servant who had so plainly and politely explained her impressions of Bertha's "situation," the long expected baby made its appearance.

A great big boy with tremendous lungs, and requiring incessant attention. It would neither sleep sound at night, nor be quiet through the day; and Mr. Herbert, with a ludicrous feeling of astonishment, found himself occasionally requested to "hold the baby," while Bertha was either snatching a short rest or "extremely busy" by her own account.

The young nurse Bertha had engaged was quite as devoid of experience as her mistress; and the latter, whose sole and small knowledge of babies was derived from occasional visits to the Haughton nursery, exacted from her one domestic the various habits she thought quite essential to the well-being of the baby, and which she forgot had taken the energies of three individuals to perform at Haughton. Now, that baby was bathed and dressed, and taken out for a walk, and redressed and bathed again!

Every cry from the child sent Bertha flying into the nursery, to the entire discomposure of the nurse's temper and her own nerves. Every new and wonderful theory upon the subject of infants was seized upon eagerly; and every female friend she had, who, being a mother of longer standing than herself, felt entitled to offer "practical advice," poured it upon her: how the unhappy child was to be fed—what it was to eat, and what to avoid. No wonder it roared; but being of a thriving nature, he did manage to thrive, in spite of the combination against him.

In the meantime, its advent did Frank a great deal of good; and though its noise disturbed the house, it was a new opening to both husband and wife, and drew out the best qualities of each after a time.

On Frank the effect was greater and happier at present than on Bertha. Poor Bertha, like many another woman, had given herself credit for evenness of temper, for high and even heroic qualities; but she had not calculated upon the effect of broken rest and perpetual fatigue, and she had not sufficient appetite to enjoy the indifferently cooked dinners provided by the "temporary" she had engaged. Just when her strength needed most keeping up, she had nothing to meet it with, and the weak feeling of *never* wishing to exert herself deterred her from the long walks to which she had been looking forward. Her temper was no longer calm or even, and she was neither bright nor cheerful, but dispirited, and even dull. It must be owned that Frank, when he had sighed for sympathy, and wished that Bertha would take a less bright view of their position, had not taken into account how different his home would be if the high spirit he in his first anxiety had felt so uncongenial were to be entirely tamed; but he was so terribly anxious now about their affairs—so taken up with preparing the whole of his accounts to meet Mr. Carter's inspection, that if he did not appreciate her low spirits he was too busy to say so.

One day, when Bertha was alone, Mr. Carter was announced. She was so delighted that he had come, so pleased that *now* there would be a solution of their difficulties, that she somewhat astonished him by the warmth of her reception. His whole idea of her was as a somewhat fine lady, who would probably make an extravagant wife for his friend Frank Herbert. The tangled accounts of her money had perhaps naturally enough prejudiced him a little against *her*, which, though unjust, was only what might be expected. He had heard she was handsome, but he had never taken to account what sort of beauty hers was; and was so conscious that he had never done her justice that he was now completely at a disadvantage.

Mr. Carter himself was a tremendous disappointment to Bertha, as far as manner and appearance went. Was it possible that the blushing, hesitating, and apparently shy man before her, was the clever, talented lawyer, that for old friendship's sake continued to Frank the interest he had had in his father?

Few people did so much injustice to themselves as Mr. Carter did, except when actually engaged in matters of business; *then* all nervous shyness disappeared—then his clear-headedness, and the concise forms of expression overpowered all the embarrassment of manner which was with him constitutional; and to those who up to that moment had *only* known him as a fussy and nervous little man, blushing like a girl, and hardly looking up, it was a complete surprise to find him scanning their countenances, and turning their ideas inside out, before they knew where they were, the moment that business was really entered upon.

He had come down to see Frank Herbert, fully prepared to find him in miserable spirits, and his wife overwhelmed with their prospects; he had given Bertha credit for neither sound sense, nor anything, except a fair share of personal beauty, which she doubtless looked upon as an excuse for running Frank into all kinds of extravagance. He had never heard anything about her that led to him fancy she had more than a superficial sort of talent; and he felt ashamed of all he had thought, when he saw the excessive simplicity of her dress, and the sweet, bright face, that bespoke so much more than " superficial talent."

After a few very common-place remarks, a dead pause ensued. Bertha did not wish to begin about their troubles without Frank; and besides, she thought Mr. Carter was the proper person to take the initiative.

The relief was great to both, when Mr. Herbert arrived in time for dinner; and Bertha's face brigthened when she saw how her husband's expression altered, and her spirits rose at the prospect of something definite; anything was better than watching Frank's gloomy face, and conjecturing the wildest things imaginable.

She was so perfectly ignorant of business, and nothing unpleasant had ever come before her! When Frank looked so sad, and spoke in a general, vague, and totally incomprehensible way of being ruined, it conveyed to her a general idea of being imprisoned, or begging, or something perfectly and utterly wretched.

Then gleams of brightness flitted across her mind: at this juncture of their affairs, she would come forward unknown to Frank, she would give music lessons, or (as she did not quite see how she was to get pupils) she would paint pictures, which would fetch fabulous prices; some day her pictures would be so famous, that being by this time very rich indeed, owing entirely to her own exertions, Frank would wish to possess one of these celebrated pictures— and then she saw him breathless with astonishment, learning that all this time, she, his Bertha, had been the means of turning the scales in their favour. She could not quite explain to herself, how Frank was to be employed all this time, and how she was to account to him for the wealth which had contributed to their general happiness to so great a degree; but all that was going much farther into the question than was at all necessary at present.

Building "castles in the air," is considered a very reprehensible employment by a great many very excellent people; it is, no doubt, not very profitable, and may do a great deal of harm if constantly indulged in; but what a weary, dreary time some people would have, if for ever they were to live *only* in the present, be painfully aware of a colourless life, and be perpetually alive to troubles which they hardly feel now, because they see themselves in the future without them!

If people (even those who speak so strongly upon the duty of taking a more realistic view of everything) were to pause occasionally, and analyse their feelings, they would be startled to find how much of their cheerfulness and happiness is the result of a future perpetually expected!

Of course those who have nothing but sunshine in their lives, cannot enter into this, their great difficulty is in properly appreciating what is theirs now; but the sunshiny people are comparatively few in number, and being able to look forward hopefully, in other words, being sanguine, is a great blessing.

Dinner passed off very well, taking all things into consideration. Mr. Carter, totally unaccustomed to the society of women, thought Bertha perfectly charming. He considered that Frank had shown the most wonderful forbearance in not insisting more upon her perfections than he had done, and found himself enjoying her amusing views of things and people, without a shadow of remembrance of money matters, or disagreeables of any kind.

He was quite sorry when she left the room, and he had to turn his attention to the business that had brought him down.

Frank drew his chair near the fire, on the side where Mr. Carter was sitting, and began by thanking him warmly for his kindness in coming to them. "I am so very anxious to know how we stand exactly; there is much that I cannot understand," he said. "Have you seen Mr. Flipson?"

"I have," said Mr. Carter—"Rascal! I have seen the will or rather the memorandum, seen your marriage settlements, and various other documents—and here I am."

"Well!" ejaculated Frank, breathlessly.

"How much exactly have you of your own, including everything?" asked Mr. Carter.

"Exactly three hundred pounds a year," answered Frank; "the sale of my commission——"

"Never mind details just now. That's all, is it? Three hundred pounds a year. Well, I'm afraid you're in a mess."

"In a mess?" said Frank, anxiously.

"In a most confounded mess!" said Mr. Carter, energetically.

Frank was silent.

"Serves you right," continued Mr. Carter, "for going to Flipson, a scoundrel, who does nothing but dirty work no one else will undertake! Why, on earth, could you not come to me, or to some respectable member of our profession?"

"Simply because Mr. Germayne insisted that I should not do so," answered Frank; "he said serious inconveniences would be the immediate consequence of his allowing any stranger to look into his affairs."

"And this never made you suspicious that something was wrong?" asked Mr. Carter.

"No," said Frank. "How should I ever dream of Mr. Germayne's having any other motive but the one he stated."

"And Sir Luke never warned you?" continued Mr. Carter.

"Sir Luke told me to be guarded," returned Frank; "but I fancied (and so did my wife) that Sir Luke was too strongly prejudiced against Mr. Germayne, to be a fair judge, their characters are so dissimilar.

"Very! I should hope," said Mr. Carter, drily; "and my letter of course did nothing either. Humph! Then why go to Flipson?"

"Mr. Germayne named him," answered Frank; "he said *he* knew all about his affairs, that he was his man of business, and he made it a *sine quâ non* that he should do everything he suggested, indeed, that we should wait a year, or some more indefinite time, but we had already waited too long!"

"And you have no papers—no security of any kind for your wife's money?"

"Nothing."

"Just as I thought. Bless me! what a set of fools! No sum specified! so much waste paper. What a rascal Germayne is, to be sure! And here you are, with a child already, and the probability of a round dozen in no time!" and Mr. Carter got up and walked about the room, muttering to himself.

"Do you know what you have done?" he said, suddenly stopping and looking at Frank.

"No," said that unhappy individual. "When? What do you mean?"

"You have signed *a release*, and your wife, too!" said Mr. Carter. "So Mr. Germayne has made himself safe, whatever happens."

"I never signed any such thing," said Frank, indignantly.

"Here is a copy; read it at your leisure," said Mr. Carter, throwing down a paper on the table, and sitting down again. "Now, as shortly as I can, I will tell you the history of your wife's money. When her father succeeded to the property he had been a widower for some years. At the time of his marriage there were no less than five lives (and good ones) between him and the succession; consequently, in his settlements, there was no provision made for younger children from the estate. There was one thousand pounds settled on the children of his marriage, and that still belongs to your wife. When Sir Clement found himself in possession of the estate, he naturally resolved to settle a larger sum on his only child, and found some difficulty in doing so, because the estate passing from cousin to cousin, had been encumbered and burthened in every possible way. It had been no one's interest to nurse it. Unfortunately he asked Mr. Germayne's advice. Mr. Germayne suggested an insurance on Sir Clement's life as being his easiest way of leaving a legacy to his daughter, but recommended its being done as quietly as possible, in case some of the creditors (of whom Sir Clement had a good many) should object to his paying the large yearly sum necessary for such an insurance at his time of life. Sir Clement consented, and was weak enough to leave the whole affair in Mr. Germayne's hands. Mr. Germayne undertook to manage it all; it is *my* belief that Sir Clement paid the interest regularly, but—the office never received it. I have ascertained that a proposal for insuring Sir Clement's life for a sum of ten thousand pounds was once entertained, but it was never carried out. In one letter (evidently left by accident among Mr. Germayne's other papers) Sir Clement refers to his anxiety about the non-arrival of any receipt or acknowledgment of the interest (amount not specified) on the insurance of his life for his daughter's benefit; and this was the clue I had. I cross-questioned and badgered Flipson, till, out of his lies, I laid hold of the truth, and made him show me the memorandum, signed by Sir Clement, but not witnessed, of which I have brought you a copy, and which distinctly desires Mr. Germayne to see that an insurance on his life for ten thousand pounds should be invested, so as to give his daughter four per cent.; and at the back of the memorandum the name of the office is written out in full."

Frank Herbert sat listening intently and eagerly, but he would not interrupt Mr. Carter by a word.

"Now," continued Mr. Carter, "among the various papers you and your wife put your signatures to, and which you probably imagined to be part of the marriage settlement, you have both signed a paper, which, in simple but conclusive terms, says that you are both perfectly satisfied with the way in which (though not legally bound to do so) Mr. Germayne has fulfilled Sir Clement's wishes, and that you release him entirely from any further obligations, &c."

Poor Frank started up and uttered an indignant exclamation.

"You now know your position," continued Mr. Carter; "you cannot claim a farthing from Mr. Germayne, and he has plunged into so many speculations that it is not likely he will come forward to do anything which the fear of the world and its opinion would perhaps have made him do. In short, if Flipson's word is good for anything, he will probably be TOO ILL even to resume his place in parliament next session." Mr. Carter came up to the fireplace and poked the fire vigorously.

Frank did not speak.

"Have you many bills?" inquired Mr. Carter, as he sat down again by the table.

"I hardly know," said the unfortunate young man; "we have not lived up to our supposed income; this furniture is our own —it is paid for. We can sell it (for, of course, we must leave this house), and that will fetch something."

"Not much," said Mr. Carter, laconically; "it is all very pretty, no doubt; but, unfortunately, taste is a fancy article, and second-hand things always go for half their original price—indeed, often less than that."

"If there was anything I could do!" exclaimed Frank, in a tone of despair.

"Plenty to be done," said Mr. Carter, cheerfully; "but we will talk over all that to-morrow. Now, what you have to do is to go upstairs and talk this over with your wife. She has a right to know everything, and it will do you good. Yours is not the temperament to brood over miseries without sympathy. I have quantities of letters to write, so I will wish you 'good night,' and go straight to my own room;" and, glad to have had the whole thing out, the kind-hearted little man bustled out of the room.

CHAPTER XV.

KNOWING THE WORST.

WHEN Bertha Haughton had accepted Mr. Francis Herbert, her notions on the subject of the poverty he spoke of had, as we have before noticed, been of the vaguest imaginable description. Carriages, horses, a French cook, powdered footmen, and the usual paraphernalia of a large establishment, had simply represented to her imagination the one, with the conviction that an opera box and diamonds (which so many people believe are so coveted by a girl, and which, as a rule, a girl appreciates so little) would not be among those things of her life.

The opposite side of the question she

knew positively nothing about. Poverty might mean anything, and she was surprised to find how much they might do if they confined their expenses to a proper limit. It is quite true that it took her a little time to reconcile herself to the indifferent cookery and indifferent servants. She hated their noisy voices, and the perpetual want of manner, which annoyed her, and was at variance with the whole habit of her previous life. But except in this, Frank was wrong when he imagined that his wife pined for anything beyond what they had believed to be their right.

A girl who has never been out anywhere, and whose whole idea of a London season is derived from overdrawn pictures by some acquaintance and the gossip of some morning papers, pines far more to take her share of the amusements announced, wishes far more eagerly to be in "society," than a girl who, like Bertha, knew it all by heart and was completely satiated with it. While

Miss Smith or Miss Jones felt that they would give anything they possessed to have gone to the brilliant party of the Duchess of Moneylands, Bertha knew by experience that her parties were the dullest imaginable things, the Duchess herself extremely commonplace, and that her party had probably been anything *but* brilliant.

All things that bear simply a fictitious value lose on a closer acquaintance; and Bertha knew the whole routine too well—had engaged and been loved, like hundreds of other girls, and had no more regret for the old life than if it was still within her reach.

But her husband—little imagining that his own reverse had acted so painfully upon her, and that she was tormenting herself with frightful and impossible things, simply because he had never talked about it all, and his look of extreme wretchedness led her to fancy that there was not a grain of hope left—had not the slightest idea that the one thing that tried her more than anything else was an idea that his devoted affection for her no longer existed, at least in the same degree. It was with a heavy heart, therefore, that poor Frank reflected how, if she had missed her old comforts so much up to the present time, what was her future life likely to be with less than half the income they expected? He did not dare to think about it any longer, and he went upstairs in a mood almost of desperation.

Bertha saw his face, and knew directly that something was wrong.

She stirred up the fire to promote cheerfulness, and drawing his own favourite armchair forwards, sat down on a stool beside him. The expression of utter misery upon his face went to her heart; and she resolved that, come what might, she would command her feelings and endeavour to comfort him.

He intended to tell her quietly, but he felt too much to trust himself to speak.

"What have you done with Mr. Carter?" was his wife's first question, and she added, "I see he has brought you very bad news; will you not talk to me about it?"

"My poor Bertha," exclaimed her husband, "it is all over; we are ruined!"

Bertha felt choked. "I do not know exactly what you mean by being ruined," she said, to her great satisfaction, in a perfectly steady voice.

"Mr. Germayne has behaved like a scoundrel. Your money is gone; there is nothing, absolutely nothing, left!" said Mr. Herbert, his indignation rising as he spoke.

"And yours," said his wife, quietly—"is yours also gone?"

"I have but three hundred a year," said Frank.

"I know perfectly well," returned Bertha; "but if you have that I do not know why you talk of being ruined. We shall not be penniless."

"You do not understand, Bertha," he said, impatiently. "What will three hundred a year be to us? As it is, I *know* that you have felt your position a hard one. Now what must it be?—it *is* ruin!"

"We must go to law," said Bertha, "and get the money back."

"We cannot," exclaimed Mr. Herbert; and he explained to his wife how hopelessly they were placed.

It was long before Bertha could understand it: her uncle, that proud reticent man, behave in this wretchedly dishonourable way! Herself scrupulous, as all of her class, it was at first *impossible* to realize or credit what Mr. Germayne had done; there must be some mistake! Pretending affection, expressing sympathy for her as an orphan, and then this!

"Is this all the worst?" she asked her husband. "Have you left nothing untold —is this *really all?*"

"Why, what can be worse?" said Frank,

almost provoked at her excessive calmness, and explaining it to himself by crediting her with a very slow comprehension of their position.

"There might be many things worse," said Bertha; "*we* have done nothing dishonourable."

"I think," said Frank, with all the calmness of despair, "that your best plan will be to go to your aunt, Lady Cecil, with baby, whilst I arrange things; and perhaps some of your relations will give you a home for a time."

"And leave you here?" said his wife, bitterly, while the tears that her prospects had not forced from her rained over her face. "Oh, Frank——"

"Poor darling," said Frank, sadly, as he drew her head upon his shoulder. "I must try and get some appointment; I will go abroad and make money somehow. This must be a terrible trial for you."

"You surely do not fancy I care so much

for the money?" exclaimed Bertha, in indignant surprise, as she started up; and then she told him everything: how she felt his reverse, and suspected his changed affection—all her conjectures and misery. She was so indignant with her husband for imagining her so dependent for her happiness upon surrounding circumstances, that he was forced to repent, and make a thousand promises of future entire trust and confidence.

With a weight lifted off their hearts, it was more as if they had gained than lost a fortune. "We will care for nothing so we are together," murmured Bertha, as, having fully discussed everything, including their future plans, they sat together late, forgetting the time and everything else; and Frank's face beamed as he turned it towards her, and pressed her to his heart.

CHAPTER XVI.

THE TANGLED SKEIN UNRAVELLED.

In our last chapter we left husband and wife romantically expressing their devotion to each other, and their wish for perpetual companionship.

Bertha, with her generous feelings quickened by the discovery of her husband's thoughtfulness for her, was in a subdued and tender mood—that put the finishing stroke to Mr. Carter's admiration and appreciation of her.

She deferred so prettily to her husband's sentiments, was so gentle in her disagreement with Mr. Carter upon some subject he rather took to heart, her lovely eyes had such a look of soft regret in them that she certainly appeared to the greatest advantage.

The increased cheerfulness of both was not a matter of any surprise to Mr. Carter.

He knew the world well enough to understand the relief—it was knowing the worst; and he did not over-estimate the way in which Bertha had taken the intelligence of her lessened prosperity.

Mr. Carter understood far better than Frank did, how long a time it takes to realize any misfortune so long as the immediate surroundings remain unchanged! It was not in a day, in a week, or even month, that the actual pressure of a very small income would be felt. Every day would add a little of its experience, would teach its lesson of self-denial. It would be the perpetual doing without things, the inability to replace what they now possessed—that would bring it home to them.

When breakfast was over Frank spoke to Mr. Carter, and asked him to spare Mr.

Germayne before his wife. "I'll not mention him at all, if I can help it," answered he; "and I see no occasion for it. What's done is done, and can't be helped. There is no use dwelling upon it."

Bertha was summoned, and they began their first great duty, looking over the accounts.

It was rather a trying thing for both Frank and his wife to go through these under the uncompromising and sharp gaze of Mr. Carter.

He, indeed, glanced at the various items merely to satisfy himself upon the subject of Bertha's supposed extravagance. His countenance was rather good when the bill for baby's trousseau came before him.

"Humph!" he said, "One hundred and fifty-four pounds seventeen shillings and sixpence. Babes, babes, babes. Well, I suppose it's all right, but (looking at Bertha over his spectacles as he spoke) it seems a very great deal to spend upon such an insignificant thing as a baby."

Bertha coloured, and Frank immediately took up the cudgels.

"Lady Haughton said that baby's outfit would probably cost five hundred pounds," he said, "so *I* think it very moderate; it is thought better to get a great many things at first."

"Oh, don't apologize—don't explain," exclaimed Mr. Carter, drily. "Of course Lady Haughton knows all about it."

In spite of this bill, however, on the whole the investigation was satisfactory. Allowing the Herberts to have received the income they expected, and to which they had a right, they had not exceeded it.

"You are quite sure these are all?" he said. "No milliner's bills, eh?"

"I have none," said Bertha; and noticing his look of surprise, she added, "you must remember my trousseau is not yet worn out."

Mr. Carter was satisfied, and pleased by her frankness—showed that he was both, by the increased kindness in tone and manner.

As they stood at present, a few hundred pounds would clear them, and Mr. Carter promised to think it all over and see what could be done; and having seen all he wished to see for himself, he hurried back to London.

The Herberts were to leave the cottage and find some place less expensive, where they might live on their reduced income more easily.

It is one of those facts which every one, placed in a similar position, becomes aware of—that if any one happens, even for a short time, to be (however little) in need of "a little help" from his friends, and allows it to appear, his friends immediately rally round him, not to afford "assistance," but to bring the unprosperous and unhappy being to a due sense of the enormity of his crime in venturing to be so unprosperous.

Those relations that became aware of the position of the Herberts showed their affection very strongly in this way:—They deluged these two with sound advice, solemn words of warning upon the consequences that inevitably follow "extravagance," reproached Bertha, and found fault with Frank, did everything in short but help them!

But to comfortable, well-disposed, indolent people, it must be very disagreeable to feel that you are probably expected to put yourself a little out of your way, and that you have not the faintest idea of so doing. There are a great many people who have had no experience at all of any trouble, and to whom the loaves and fishes of this life come so easily, that they cannot receive the idea of trouble coming, as it did to the Herberts, without their being in the least to blame! These considered themselves entitled to write to Bertha and her husband in the irritating tone of superiority, that nothing but the consciousness of a fat balance at their banker's could bestow.

Bertha took a great deal of unnecessary exertion; she wrote and explained, and fumed and worked herself into a perfect fever. She might have spared herself the trouble. It was the old story over again.

Her friends and his too had made up their minds from the very first that they would get themselves into a mess, and it was just what they had done. They had justified all their predictions, and day after day brought letters, reproachful, pitying, and anything but sympathizing. One only out of Bertha's friends sent them substantial help, and that friend neither offered advice nor insisted upon finding fault.

By degrees their plans were made, and they prepared to leave their first home.

It was only natural that Bertha should regret leaving it; it was endeared to her in many ways, and as the birth-place of her boy, her first-born, she felt quite a pang when she found their departure a settled thing.

There is no use in dwelling upon the various methods by which Mr. Carter succeeded in extricating them from their difficulties. He managed it after being once or twice defeated in his attempts by the utter want of sympathy that distinguished some, and the want of confidence in others, who had taken up the popular view of "the Herberts getting into a mess so early in the day," and who considered that the fact of their wanting any help was the most brilliant possible reason why they should have none!

And so at last they departed, and their pretty cottage, falling into other hands, was immediately pulled about, and "improved" beyond recognition.

CHAPTER XVII.

CHANGE OF SCENE.

IN a remote country, where railroads as yet were a pleasure to come, the Herberts found a home.

Bertha had so strenuously insisted upon carrying all her sorrows and shrunken fortunes as far as possible from the ken of her relations and friends, that Frank had yielded the point; but he was afraid that she would find it difficult to reconcile herself to the complete solitude she chose. His wife, however, spoke in such an enthusiastic way of the new sense of her duties that had dawned upon her, and drew such a glowing picture of the way in which she meant to fulfil those duties, that he was hardly to be blamed for being convinced that in reality all her tastes lay in a hermitage, and that he had been completely mistaken in imagining her fond of society! Action was always pleasant to her, and in the relief of being liberated from their pressing difficulties, Bertha felt capable of every sort of sacrifice—always excepting the small sacrifices that arose at the moment.

The fact is, that there are a good many people who really can make up their minds to a grand act of self-denial, who let slip past them, as unworthy of notice, a thousand trifling little things in reality of much greater importance in the long run. Bertha, for instance, was able to resign without a sigh an expensive dress she wished for, or make up her mind to do without some much greater luxury beyond her reach, but she thought it quite unnecessary to get up one moment sooner than she felt inclined, and never thoroughly understood what a daily trial her unpunctual habits were to her husband, or how much the discomfort of the household was to be attributed to her way of never coming downstairs two days together at the same time.

At Haughton, breakfast was nominally at ten o'clock; but Sir Luke breakfasted early in his own room; and therefore no one cared about being in time. Some lounged in at one time, some at another—it did not signify. Bertha *would* not see that with two or three servants—instead of two or three dozen—this would not do.

Frank was much happier at first than he had been for some time; it was an immense relief to him knowing the worst. Then he was very busy: the rose-trees, in profusion and disorder, claimed his attention in turn with shelves innumerable that were wanted all over the house, and he was employed from morning to night. He had also applied to all his relations and friends likely to help him, about getting some employment for him, though what employment he was exactly fitted for he would have been puzzled to tell. However, the prospect of being occupied served for the present to keep his mind easy, and the change of air had done his health good, so that he was on the whole cheerful.

To Bertha the trial was very much greater.

She was essentially one of those people easily influenced by the "ugly things" Frank had so shunned when they had first started in the capacity of householders.

It is true that she really could make the best of any materials she had; but if she had no materials——

With the best will in the world, she was influenced in the morning when her eyes opened upon a very ugly carpet that did *not* cover the room; her dressing-table was small, and would not hold her pretty things; her washing-stand was hideous in every particular; and the very paper on the walls was one of those frightful ones which must be the result of a bad bilious attack acting on the designer's imagination. It had spots of something intended for a rose, with a perpetual bud sticking out upon one side. How those spots afflicted Bertha! Her pretty and luxurious rooms at Haughton would rise to her recollection as she dressed before the little scrap of looking-glass that distorted without reflecting her whole face!

Very foolish, of course, and much to be condemned by all sensible practical people; but she could not help it;—to her credit it must be remembered that she never allowed Frank to know it. His imagination was not one to be easily affected simply by a frightful paper. He thought the whole thing in very bad taste, but having settled this point he allowed it to fall into oblivion, accepting it as part of the life which their present position entailed upon them. As it could not be helped, there was no use dwelling upon it!

Of course, there are some people whose minds are so nobly and magnificently proportioned, that the fact of being uncomfortable would be delightful to them, as a proof placed in their power to show the object of their affections how entirely they are by their blissful state of mind raised above these things.

Bertha was only becoming every day more fond of her husband. She was only *learning* to appreciate him, and her increasing affection showed itself in the very useful way of not damping his energies, or lowering his spirits. He was constitutionally and naturally liable to depression, and Bertha, though she did not get up in time, and was not at all perfect, or anything like it, was learning her lesson well, and managed to keep all her domestic troubles out of his sight.

And they were many! She had enough

to do, and though half conscious that most of her grievances were caused by her own inexperience, she did not know how easily she might have lessened them.

Like most girls, brought up in a house with a multitude of servants, it took her a long time to discover how easily a couple could get through all that was required of them. She lived in the perpetual fear of over-working them, and the most flagrant acts of carelessness she excused to herself by dwelling upon " all they had to do."

They naturally availed themselves of this weakness on the part of a mistress, whom they rather despised for it.

Peace, therefore, at present was the portion of the Herberts, but unfortunately it was again broken upon.

Miss Mary Thurston had been living at Eppington ever since Bertha's marriage, sending constant specimens of her industry to her, in the shape of baby socks, and various intricate pieces of knitting for Bertha herself, who wondered over them a little as impossible feats to her, and who rewarded Miss Mary by letters, giving full and minute particulars of the infant Hercules, whose achievements and intelligence, "*ways*" good, pretty, or clever, were dwelt upon by a mother who had very little else to occupy her, than watching with astonishment every progressive step. Miss Mary thoroughly enjoyed these letters; to her, it was almost as much a matter of interest as Baby's remarkable attempts to stand upright, and his original manner of expressing his satisfaction at other times, were to Bertha herself.

Not, therefore, without a slight feeling of pique did Bertha now find that two letters from her had been unnoticed for an unusual length of time, and she wondered if she had exhausted her friend's sympathy, when she received a letter that filled her with regret and sorrow.

Poor Miss Mary was, alas! also a victim

to Mr. Germayne's plausible representations; she and Miss Priscilla had invested through him all their earnings; the increased income that this step had at first brought them, which had placed them in comfort, had now totally ceased; and at a time of life when both had hoped to remain free from care, and independent, they were both again thrown upon the mercy of the world—*they* really were penniless!

It was only to be expected that Bertha would feel this for them as being a bitter aggravation of all her own loss, but when she found that this blow, so totally unexpected and terrible in its effects, had so acted upon poor Miss Priscilla's nerves and enfeebled frame, that she had sunk under it, and after lingering a week or two, rendered doubly bitter to her sister by her perpetual reproaches, she had died. Bertha felt as if her own grievance sank to nothing in comparison.

If Bertha had not hitherto fully discovered the better parts of her husband's character, his sympathy now would have opened her eyes.

He felt both for Miss Mary and for his wife. Nothing could have been a greater addition to Bertha's personal regrets. He did not confine his sympathy to words; to Bertha's infinite surprise and satisfaction, he suggested Miss Mary's being invited there immediately, and proved, that by a slight alteration in their arrangements, they could receive her without inconvenience.

Poor Miss Mary! the tears she shed on the receipt of the joint invitation, were as much of joy on their account, as of regret that she could not feel it right to accept it; for she recognised in Bertha's letter the far deeper love she bore her husband; every line written in her own, frank, hearty way, betrayed that intense affection which Miss Mary had justly at first doubted.

She wrote, however, warmly and gratefully, to decline the proposed kindness; indeed she had already made arrangements to receive some daily pupils at her own house; and though she spoke feelingly of her sister's illness and death, it was evident that already her spirits felt the relief and freedom which her death gave her, and for the present Bertha felt she could do nothing save sympathize and remember her, by continuing those letters which gave almost equal pleasure to both.

CHAPTER XVIII.

A MODEL RECTOR.

THE village of Dollington where the Herberts had pitched their tent was absolutely destitute of all kind of society; there was not even the usual old lady who supplies weak tea and scandal *ad lib*.

Even the doctor lived at some little distance, and both the rectory and the church were at least one mile off.

In the clergyman Bertha had hoped to find a companion for her husband, and a friend for herself; but the moment that saw the acquaintance begin put an end for ever to any such expectations.

A red-faced, burly man, with a consequential manner, a loud laugh, and a noisy voice, speaking much of crops and stock, and evidently considering himself an authority upon *all* subjects—such was Mr. Doall.

The first time they called at the cottage, the Herberts were out walking; but anxious to make the acquaintance of the only neighbours the place afforded, Bertha persuaded her husband to accompany her in a few days to return the visit, and they walked up to the rectory together.

Such a rectory! a sort of chaos! partly unroofed, partly rebuilt; stones and bricks in one place, mortar in another, planks evidently the worse for weather, a wall begun and left unfinished, no workman about, not a sound to be heard that indicated progress.

The whole place looked poverty-stricken!

They knocked, and waited a considerable time—all was still. Frank knocked again (the bell-wire was there, but it was broken); still no answer.

What were they to do? The door was open, so he advanced along a dark stone passage, and soon heard a hubbub of voices in a room quite at the end of the passage. Thinking it the only thing to do, he knocked with his stick loudly on the passage floor.

A door was suddenly opened, and a number of voices chorused out—" Come in —come in!"

Frank advanced and announced himself.

In a small, very low room, sat the family party, the fumes of wine and onions proclaimed dinner to be just over, and he apologized and began to retreat; but if he calculated upon an escape, it was because he had necessarily but an imperfect knowledge of the Doall family.

Energy was their characteristic, male and female. It was astonishing, indeed, by their own account, what an immense amount of energy each member of the family possessed.

Catching from his apology something

about Mrs. Herbert, they rose tumultuously, and rushed to the door, where they captured her.

The Herberts' explanation of their not having succeeded in making themselves heard, was received with exclamations of surprise in every key of the strong family voice.

It was wonderful! perfectly wonderful! How "Mary" had not heard the knock—what "Mary" could have been doing, and why "Mary" should have been invisible, were discussed in anything but semi-tones and with great zest.

"That *we* did not hear you is simple enough," said the most voluble of the sisters, a woman with a decided manner, and a very provincial accent, with a multiplication of energy in her whole person. "My brother Philip was in one of his amusing veins to-day, and when *he* begins to tell anecdotes, we are apt to get very uproarious!"

Bertha murmured something about being no doubt a merry family party.

"Well," rejoined Miss Betsy (for so was the loudest-voiced one called), "so we are! myself and two sisters live here; then my two nieces, remarkably clever, amusing girls they are! then my brothers are quite wonderfully clever; Philip in particular. If you want any advice, you can come to *him* with perfect confidence—few people know so much about everything as does Philip."

"Is that the rector's name?" inquired Bertha.

"Yes; dear me, I quite forgot the possibility of any one in this part of the world not knowing his name!"

"Is it a large parish?" was Bertha's next question.

"Yes, very large; and he has the parish adjoining."

"It is a singular thing," said Miss Betsy (as if she was stating a very commonplace fact, and quite an agreeable one), "but though the parish is large, he has no parishioners."

"No parishioners!" echoed Bertha, extremely surprised.

"No parishioners—all dissenters—some one thing, some another; it lightens the week's labours very much; but my brother works *very* hard on Sundays."

"And the church—who fills it? Is *it* deserted?" asked Bertha.

"Yes," chimed in another sister, "and if you've any Puseyite notions, Mrs. Herbert, you will be shocked with the look of the church; it is dreadfully out of repair!"

"I suppose it will be repaired some day," said Bertha, without caring to discuss the merits or demerits of Puseyism with her new acquaintances. "What is the reason of its being so dilapidated?"

"Some dispute about church rates," said Miss Betsy, confidently; "and another thing," she added, lowering her voice a little, "my brother Philip understands church architecture so thoroughly, that it would be very painful to him to have anything patched or inferior, so he is carving the restorations himself."

"Is he really?" said Bertha, who, among her various other accomplishments, had more than once carved some rather clever figures, &c. "It is a very pleasant amusement."

"Ah! you know something about it," said Miss Betsy, patronizingly; "that is very fortunate. I am sure my brother will be delighted to give you some hints."

Bertha was conscious of not feeling properly grateful. "You are not well off for neighbours?" she said.

"Oh, we are really quite independent of neighbours," exclaimed three or four voices all at once. "We are a host in ourselves."

"Are the people very poor about here?' inquired Bertha, who was getting rather at a loss for something to say.

"No, not at all," answered Miss Betsy, decidedly; "it is quite a singular fact, but there really are *no* poor in this parish."

"That certainly is very curious," said Bertha; "why do the cottages look so wretched and miserable? They *look* poor; but perhaps that is because they are so horribly dirty and untidy."

"There *are no poor*," insisted Miss Betsy, who had evidently taken possession of her visitor. "They are a very ungrateful and discontented set, and they grumble a great deal; but all the old people are on the parish, consequently they are all provided for!"

"I have already made acquaintance with a good many," said Bertha, "and they seem to want help of all sorts."

All the family raised their hands and eyes, and allowed brother Philip to speak.

"I think it probable," he said, with a look of suppressed amusement, that Bertha thought extremely disagreeable, "that you will soon find them out; if you encourage them, they will never leave you alone."

"Of course, you must know them better than I do," said Bertha, coldly; "but it is new to me to find a place where there are no poor, to whom a little assistance is necessary."

"Of course, if you intend to be *benevolent*," said Mr. Doall, with an air of patronizing superiority which was inexpressibly provoking, "you will have no difficulty in finding 'objects.' I'll undertake to get up at least half-a-dozen pet old women for you immediately, all provided with a thousand wants; but I trust you will not begin what will *quite* spoil the parish—indiscriminate assistance. I very much dislike giving anything—in fact, as a rule, I never do; if they come to me I send them to the parish, and for a long time now I have never seen any one."

"It is a pity," said Frank, "that some one does not look after their houses a little.

I never saw such miserable huts anywhere else."

"Oh! my dear sir!" said the model rector, "they would not thank you to improve their houses; they are very fond of their mud walls; and you will soon get accustomed to them."

Bertha fervently hoped they would not. She could not reconcile herself to the views Mr. Doall accepted and set forth. Her ideas about the poor were womanly, impossible, and perhaps Utopian. She felt that there was no necessity in this country for such poverty; and on taking leave of the rectory and its inhabitants, she warmly argued it all with her husband.

That part of the country, in truth, was in a very wretched state. The people, scantily fed, had no energy, and no wish to alter the existing state of things.

The wages were the lowest possible. The whole land was divided into small holdings, that had been, and still were, occupied by proprietors whose forefathers had lived and died there for centuries. Not one of the million schemes of improvement had yet penetrated there; labour was totally unassisted by any one of the improvements mechanical science has brought to bear upon agriculture; the unkindly and stiff soil was *scratched* every year, and the scanty crops told their own tale.

"Want of capital!" said Bertha, when Frank had in some measure enlightened her as to the great want in the place; and she reflected, sadly enough, that if nothing would really improve the country and the people except capital, things must remain as they were as far as she was concerned. But, in spite of Mr. Doall, she meant to do what she could to alleviate distress; and the people around soon recognised a friend, and the sympathy they called forth did her infinite good. How much our happiness depends upon ourselves, was a lesson Bertha was learning day by day.

CHAPTER XIX.

A NEW LIGHT ON THE SUBJECT OF CLERICAL DUTIES.

Sunday came, and Bertha and her husband went to church.

A church! No description of it can come up to the reality! Desolation reigned supreme; and neglect asserted itself in its every aspect. In spite of some straw thatch inserted into the roof, the sky here and there was visible through it.

Wreaths of ivy, with its fresh green leaves, clambered up inside the walls, as if in mockery of the want of shelter they afforded. Those walls, within which were doubtless at one time assembled many who had helped to erect what must have been a beautiful building in its youth, were now all manner of colours from damp.

Bertha and her husband were very early, and they watched with some interest the entrance of the congregation.

An elderly, heavy-featured man clamped up the aisle, and sat down without the faintest sign of reverence. Then a somewhat younger man bustled in, and began to find the places for the rector, whispering very loudly to his friend all the time, and finally descending and holding a long conversation with an old woman, bent nearly double with age. Then a long pause; and a cracked bell, pulled in a hasty and irregular way by some lad, ushered in the Doall family.

Not another person appeared. Those present happened to be dependent upon the rectory, and they slept through the service. No child's voice echoed the responses; and the scene was one so perfectly new to the Herberts, that they could hardly refrain from a whispered comment to each other.

The Doall family, of course, were there in great force, dresses, bonnets, &c., of the most exaggerated style of the last fashion.

The rector walked pompously up the aisle, and donned his surplice in a pew in full view of the congregation, then stepping into the reading-desk he began to read the service in a loud and sonorous voice, rolling out the sentences in a manner peculiarly his own, and all the more felt in a perfectly empty church. Not an attempt was made to sing any praises; there was indeed no one (except Bertha) who could have sung, as nature had been singularly niggardly to the Doall family in the way of musical ability, and the absence of even a hymn struck Bertha forcibly.

She was peculiarly alive to outward influences, and blamed herself for feeling so chilled and saddened altogether. Mr.

Doall's sermon was one peculiarly addressed to drones and idlers; taking as his text, "Whatever thy hand findeth to do," &c., he enlarged and descanted upon it in forcible language, reminding his hearers of the parable of the talents, and the penalty inflicted upon the unprofitable servant, and winding up with immense energy, with the quotation about not being "hearers only——" He gave the benediction with an amount of earnestness thrown into his voice that would have befitted a patriarch blessing his people probably for the last time. "Surely I must have misjudged this man," thought Bertha, as she was leaving church. "It is surely impossible for a man to preach in that way, unless his conscience was perfectly clear.

The church outside was sadly in keeping with the interior; the roof, as already stated, was partly thatched with straw; rank grass and nettles crowded up to the doors; a small iron gate was off its hinges, with a good deal of it missing; and the bank was broken down upon each side, so as to afford egress to a herd of donkeys, poor starved animals, whose only pickings were this pasturage in "God's acre," and who were only ejected during service, but at all other times found easy entrance and luxuriated there; a few wretched mud houses crowded round the church, and were disfigured by muddy puddles at every door step. This was the exterior!

To Bertha's infinite annoyance they were instantly taken possession of by all the Doall family, who, making their exit by another door, had waited for them.

"My brother has a very powerful voice," was Miss Betsy's remark the moment the greetings were over.

"Very powerful, indeed," said Bertha.

"It is quite wonderful," returned Miss Betsy; "he can read for hours without the slightest fatigue."

Bertha expressed her astonishment.

" Yes! I always find such a difference," continued Miss Betsy, in the self-satisfied family voice that Bertha was growing to hate; "when I have been away from home and return here, my brother's voice sounds so rich and full after other clergymen's voices. I *think* you must have noticed how admirably his voice fills the church!"

Bertha thought, but did not say that it was not difficult to fill a church with one's voice when it was so perfectly empty otherwise; to turn the subject, she said, "I saw no school children in church."

"Why, you see there are none," replied Miss Betsy, quite coolly.

"No school children!" exclaimed Bertha.

"No. None," rejoined her companion. "We have no parish school; there was a school some years ago, when my brother first came here, but it was a dreadful trouble. The schoolmistresses were always leaving, and were a perpetual nuisance, and my brother takes high notions of the duties of a schoolmistress, and so at last we gave it up altogether."

"And you have no Sunday-school?" inquired Bertha.

"No," answered Miss Betsy. "You see it was no use having a school for half-a-dozen children who attended irregularly, and so we gave it up long ago."

Bertha felt quite bewildered. No school! No Sunday-school. A church like a barn out of repair; and a clergyman who had no parishioners, and was nevertheless perfectly satisfied with his position! who in these days would believe that such a state of things existed! "And he preaches about drones, &c.," said Bertha, when she had shaken off the rectory party, and found herself alone with her husband.

"That sermon is always a favourite of mine," said Mr. Herbert, quietly, "and he certainly read it very well."

"How!" exclaimed Bertha, "is it not his own?"

"No. I can show it you when we get home," rejoined her husband. "I think it wise of him to read other people's sermons, as I should fancy his own might be very inferior productions."

"I think he is quite right too," said Bertha; "and though I still wonder he chose that subject to preach about, it is not quite so bad of him if he did not compose it."

"We must not judge too hastily," said Frank; "he may be a better clergyman than we fancy him at present."

"My dear, the schools," said his wife, "and those self-satisfied people; but we will not discuss them any more — drones indeed!"

CHAPTER XX.

"SCHEIDEN, SCHEIDEN TUT WEH!'

"I HAVE heard of something to do," was Frank's exclamation to his wife, one morning, a few months after their residence at the cottage. "I am only afraid it is not worth taking; but an occupation of any kind would be such a blessing!"

"What is it?" eagerly asked his wife.

"It is to go abroad, to look into some affairs that have gone wrong, and bring a delinquent to account," answered Frank. "I am to have all my expenses paid, a per centage on the money recovered, and a hundred pounds into the bargain. Carter has written about it. Some client of his asked him to find some gentleman to undertake the journey, and he thought of me. It was very kind of him, but I do not think it is worth taking."

" What part of the world is it in?—where should you have to go to?" asked Bertha, anxiously.

" China."

" China!"

" Yes. What do you think about it? You see you cannot possibly go with me."

" It is such a *very* long way off!"

" It *is* an immense journey; and I cannot bear leaving you alone in this wretched little place, and your confinement coming on and all; no, I will write to Carter, and tell him it is quite impossible, and that he has proposed the only thing I cannot possibly undertake just now; no, it is utterly out of the question."

" Pray do not think about me," said poor Bertha, with a tight feeling in her throat; " I shall do very well, and if you can make some money by going out there, it will be so very delightful. Fancy your coming home very rich indeed!"

"There is very small hope of that," rejoined her husband; "but the question is, is it right to throw away the only chance I have had put in my power of doing anything for myself."

"That is the *real* question," said his wife; "but I am quite convinced you will come home very rich—enormously rich; everybody does who goes to China."

"I happen to know several people who have been to China," replied Frank, "and who returned not even moderately well off."

"Soldiers and sailors," said she; "of course nothing would make them rich anywhere. I am thinking of people who have a great deal to do with tea, and give great dinners out there."

"I see no prospect of an appointment coming to me through the influence of any of our friends," said Frank, musingly; "we have been five months here, and have heard of nothing up till now, and I am so heartily tired of doing nothing."

"All appointments now seem to require such a perfect knowledge of one or more languages," said Bertha; "and you hate every language but your own."

"I know French quite well enough for anything," said Frank, a little impatiently, "though I do not pretend to speak it; but the fact is, that discussing my inefficiency as a linguist will not help us to decide the question of my accepting this offer of Carter's. What do you really think about it?"

"I do not know yet," said Bertha. "I have not had time to realize the thing yet. You are certainly miserable with nothing to do, and yet I cannot bear to think of your going such a great way off; and I somehow feel as if it would be wrong in our circumstances to refuse it. I am quite bewildered."

"I shall take a walk, and think it over," said Frank; "we have two or three days given us to decide about it."

"Just tell me, before you go," said Bertha, "how are you to manage Chinese accounts?"

"It has nothing to do with Chinese accounts," said her husband. "A clerk was sent out from a merchant's office to recover some money due to the firm he belonged to. It is known that he did recover it, and it amounted to a considerable sum; but he has not been heard of since. I am going (if I go) to endeavour to trace him. Do you understand now?"

So saying, he nodded to his wife, and walked off, looking more cheerful than he had done for a very long time.

The walk was taken, and the result was, that he felt he could not decline the proposal with a clear conscience. He could hardly bear to think of Bertha, alone, without a companion, a strange doctor, and everything so cheerless and miserable round her; yet when he returned home, Bertha met him so cheerfully, spoke so hopefully of her life during his absence, and held up his return home in such bright colours, that half his anxieties on her account vanished, and he wrote his grateful acceptance to Mr. Carter so cheerfully that he gained golden opinions from that worthy man.

Now that it was settled, Bertha was fully occupied with the preparations for her husband's departure.

Of course her greatest anxiety was to lessen his sorrow as much as possible, and she knew that if she once gave way—if she allowed him to guess how much she dreaded his leaving her, especially with the prospects she had, his own feelings would prompt him at once to resign all idea of leaving England. He, indeed, wished her to leave the cottage and go somewhere near some friend or relation; but Bertha wisely felt that they could ill afford this extra expense, and that it was another occasion for self-denial.

Miss Mary Thurston was making too much money where she was to be asked to leave; but she promised to come and stay at least a fortnight with Bertha, when she expected her confinement.

This was a very great comfort to both Frank and Bertha; and the latter felt that her husband needed some occupation so much, that, putting everything else out of the question, it was her duty not to stand in the way of his availing himself of this opening.

She was also (as usual) full of plans on her own account.

She had read in various novels how the heroines, after a certain number of disappointments and trials in Vol. I. triumphed in all sorts of ways in Vol. III.; sometimes, indeed, achieved the most brilliant possible success, in spite of the slight drawbacks of neither education nor natural ability, they made an immense quantity of money in various ways—drawings, work, and writing.

It was only natural to Bertha's sanguine temper to imagine herself capable of making a great deal of money in any or all of these three roads to wealth, and hundreds of pounds enclosed "with compliments and thanks," floated before her buoyant imagination!

Yes! whilst her husband was away she would do *her* part as a pleasant surprise. Music! she would compose an opera, only she just then, unfortunately, remembered that she had no piano. Drawings! how immensely her drawings had been admired by all those who had seen them. Writing! Yes, she would set about *that* directly; she would write an historical romance, and she felt sure it would be a great success. The only drawback was she had no books of reference, and she might misplace her characters in point of date, or dress them wrongly (and she meant to detail their costumes), and that would be still worse. She already had written in imagination the description of a storm, and introduced two of the principal characters, one of whom should swear by his halidom, or use some mediæval oath, and the other should always say " Gramercy;" when she reflected that on Sundays she might occupy her time very profitably by writing some good practical sermons to be published anonymously. In short, Bertha's brain so turned with these, and a few other projects, that her husband could not understand why on the eve of his departure she had suddenly resumed the gay cheerfulness so long a stranger to her.

The day of actual parting arrived. Bertha, in spite of her plans, felt it dreadfully, and nothing but the overpowering anxiety to lessen Frank's own grief enabled her to control herself.

He left, and then poor Bertha's philosophy deserted her, and her tears, almost entirely restrained for her husband's sake, found vent now that he was no longer there to be influenced by them.

Her only hope now, was soon to see him return; and in the meantime she counted the days that were to bring Miss Mary Thurston to her side. That was the prospect that kept up her spirits, and enabled her to face her coming trial with fortitude.

CHAPTER XXI.

TROUBLES AND TRIALS.

A FEW weeks passed away, and Bertha, some two months before she expected it, found herself again a mother, and of a delicate girl.

She was very ill and frightened when she found herself utterly alone, without a human being near her to whom she might look for comfort and sympathy.

Accustomed to the polished, well-bred, and refined physician who formed her idea of a doctor, she could not endure the little, dirty, snuffy, fussy, old man, who smelt of snuff and brandy, and whose nervous manner inspired no confidence, and less esteem. He was both rough and unskilful from total want of practice amongst even the poor women about.

Dr. Flapping was, indeed, a specimen of a class now fast passing away.

Bertha had not expected much, simply because when she found that the Doalls invariably descanted upon his superior merits, and quoted him upon all occasions, her mind misgave her.

His conversation was also as far from Bertha's experiences as possible. He delighted in recounting and enlarging upon the most horrible operations, in which he figured as chief performer, and if one half of his narration was to be believed, his resources in emergencies were quite enough to cause the hair of every individual member of the College of Surgeons to stand on end with horror!

Wordy, garrulous, and immensely vain, he dwelt upon his skill, and his presence of mind, till Bertha could hardly keep her countenance, and he misquoted Latin so often, that Bertha longed to present him with the correct editions of sentences familiar to her, as to most other well-educated English girls in these days.

Miss Mary Thurston could not come to her for a week or so, and Bertha felt her lonely position dreadfully.

With the best intentions in the world, she neither regained strength nor health, as she ought to have done.

The Doall family came frequently to see her, and she admitted them, as she was anxious to accept kindness where it was meant; but their visits irritated her always more than anything else. She found that their absorbing admiration for everything connected with themselves extended to their family doctor.

They dwelt upon Dr. Flapping's perfections in the face of Bertha's personal experience, and insisted upon talent that she knew too well existed entirely in their own imagination.

But how could she say anything? Was he not " consulting physician" to the Doall family; and did not brother Philip consider him an extraordinarily clever man? After this it was hopeless to get the Doall mind to admit any inferiority.

She was glad soon to feign entire recovery, and to get rid of him and the infliction of the daily visits of this " self-taught" genius.

It was unfortunate that in selecting the cottage as a residence for a few months, the Herberts had not taken its situation into consideration.

On the sloping bank of a river—nothing could be prettier than it was in the height of summer; but when the summer passed away, when November fogs were succeeded by a rainy December, the place was flooded immediately, and the incessant damp affected everyone in the vicinity.

The day that Miss Mary Thurston arrived, she was struck by Bertha's look of transparency. She was too careful to say anything to her personally, but she could not help feeling anxious about her.

It was not like Bertha to remain idle and listless, as if fairly tired out, at five o'clock in the afternoon. After the joy of meeting, and the almost hysterical fit of crying which surprised Miss Thurston, had passed away, she saw that Bertha was languid. Her eyes were bright, but they had more the brilliancy of fever than anything else. She took her hands: they were burning.

Bertha, however, did not complain of illness, and Miss Mary hoped it was all only the consequences of over-excitement while still weak.

The next morning, however, found Bertha acknowledging that she felt ill, and she remained in bed.

The luxury, the happiness, of having her old friend was quite beyond expression!

She got so ill, and was so weak, that,

finding how little confidence she had in Dr. Flapping, Miss Thurston, on her own responsibility, summoned the kind and clever doctor who had attended Bertha's first confinement. When he arrived, he found that she was suffering from a severe attack of low fever, and that the baby showed symptoms of the same illness. He remained two or three days, and left full instructions with Miss Thurston, promising to come again, if necessary.

It was almost as well that Bertha was too ill to take in all the worry and annoyances to which Miss Thurston was subjected.

Dr. Flapping called several times, but was simply told Mrs. Herbert did not wish to see him.

The Doall family were amazed and indignant!

The idea of Miss Thurston—a governess —setting herself up as a judge! What next? Their Dr. Flapping, a man who was *so* superior, to be set on one side!—a man who actually wrote "articles" for several medical papers, and that brother Philip considered so clever!

"Mrs. Herbert has made a very serious mistake," began the strong-minded sister, to Miss Mary, one day. "It is quite inconceivable her not recognising Dr. Flapping's superior abilities. I assure you, if my brother was to be taken ill, he would immediately send for Dr. Flapping. He is a very superior man."

"Perhaps he is not exactly a ladies' doctor," said Miss Thurston, anxious to say nothing disagreeable.

"Precisely what he is?" answered Miss Betsy, triumphantly. "A clever man like him can be anything. *We* consider him a particularly good ladies' doctor."

"Your experience and Mrs. Herbert's have not been quite the same," said Miss Thurston, with a feeling of great amusement.

"I beg your pardon," said Miss Betsy,

mistaking her meaning, "I think *we* have had plenty of experience!"

"I meant about babies, &c.," said Miss Mary, calmly.

Miss Betsy rose indignantly. "I cannot pretend to misunderstand you now," she said; "really, I was not aware of the turn this discussion was taking. I beg to tell you, Miss Thurston, that I consider your allusion very indecent, and not at all what we are accustomed to speak about. Of course, if anything happens to Mrs. Herbert, you are the responsible person. *We* wash our hands of the whole affair!" And, with a jerk of her whole person, the insulted lady marched off.

Miss Thurston amused Bertha by telling her this little passage-at-arms, and they agreed that it was time now to repress the exuberance of the Doall's civility; and Miss Thurston undertook to accomplish this in a manner as little wounding to their self-love as possible.

CHAPTER XXII.

REFLECTIONS.

The anxious days and nights succeeded each other with that monotony which is generally the characteristic feature of a long and wearisome illness like Mrs. Herbert's.

Incessant was the care of Miss Thurston. It is not too much to say that Bertha was the only great tie she had to life. From her childhood up till now she had been the great object of her existence, and she loved with all the concentrated affection of a really warm heart the motherless pupil, whose bright and genial nature had given to her life its greatest charm.

The child, too, was ill, and between the two she really had as much as she could manage.

In the meantime a letter came to hand from Frank: he had arrived at Shanghai, and that was all; he knew nothing of his future plans, as he had as yet communicated with no one; but the fact of his safe arrival was a great thing for Bertha. His letter, too, spoke of feeling much better than when he left England, and he gave an amusing account of some of his companions on board the steamer; altogether, the letter was cheerful, and gave Bertha's spirits the fillip they needed.

There is often a false impression upon the subject of the trial of a long illness.

Generally speaking the languor of the body which enforces rest and quiet is accompanied by a languor of the mind, which renders exertion of any kind distasteful.

Carefully nursed, her mind free from worry, all the small disagreeables of life kept from her by her friend, Bertha gratefully recognised a peace to which hitherto she had been a stranger, and she accepted the time for thought as a boon to be especially remembered and taken advantage of.

It seemed to her now that her whole life had been a continued hurry; as if till now she had never had the opportunity for reviewing her past life, for trying to become acquainted with herself.

What had become of all her schemes? Where was the activity that she was to astonish her husband with?

She had started in her married life by giving herself credit for more of the peculiar sort of fortitude which stands people in such good stead, in time of trial, than her husband. Without being what is called conceited, or unduly appreciating her personal appearance, she acknowledged now that she had felt a sort of mental superiority, because she had a very keen sense of the ridiculous, and saw the ludicrous side of life more quickly than her husband. She fancied herself the ruling spirit, and expected him to be filled with admiration for talents which she intended him to appreciate more and more every day of her life.

It is true that she was influenced much by the illness hanging about her, as we always are, and exaggerated to herself the failures and mistakes she had made. Her marriage had been a great mistake. She ought to have exercised her influence, and persuaded Frank to wait, and begin with a definite aim and employment. How different all would have been then! Her husband would have been independent of the small fortune she had lost; and if she had listened to Sir Luke, and not felt that overweening confidence in her own judgment, all this would never have happened.

Is there any one who does not at times see the past with different and humbled eyes?

Her relations, too, she was on very friendly terms with them; but she confessed that, had she taken the trouble, they might all now be her intimate friends; and again, this would have made a great difference, and Frank, instead of flying off to China, might now be calmly reposing under the shelter of a house of his own.

Then how little had she been able to contribute to her husband's comfort at home. Her domestic management had been another failure. Instead of having really studied the subject, and brought her fairly good clear head to bear upon "the trifles that form the sum of human kind," she had considered it all as beneath her talents; she had done nothing (she now thought) but "leave undone" what she ought to have done.

Miss Thurston considered that a great deal of all this self-reproach was consequent upon her darling's being ill and out of spirits.

Her views about Bertha were of the most opposite nature imaginable.

She considered that a brilliant, clever, and beautiful girl, voluntarily relinquishing all the advantages of a very good position, and the success which accompanied her in society, was a proof of a superiority that ought to be recognised far and near.

Bertha, young and fond of society, had buried herself cheerfully in a remote district, where her talents had no scope, and where her only society was a tiresome and vulgar set of people, who bored her to death.

Miss Thurston thought her perfectly wonderful; but then she had always felt that Bertha was quite fitted for a heroine; she had been tried, severely tried, and had *not* been found wanting.

Day after day she admired the way in which she made the best of everything.

Remembering Miss Priscilla's constant and wearisome complaints about the unhappy loss they had had, Bertha's way of accepting her position without murmuring became beautiful by comparison.

Miss Mary remained as long as she could,

and had the happiness of leaving Bertha better and stronger than she even hoped to leave her.

She also now daily expected to hear from Frank about his return. Mr. Carter, in forwarding remittances, had mentioned, with approbation, the exertions of Mr. Herbert, and said that, satisfied with the intelligence he had already obtained for them, the firm employing him had forwarded such directions to Mr. Herbert as would probably enable him to return to England in a shorter time than they at first expected.

So that, altogether, Bertha's future was beginning to brighten, and hope once more dawned upon her lowered and depressed spirits.

CHAPTER XXIII.

HOMEWARD BOUND.

THERE are some days given to us in spring, bright beautiful days, when the mere consciousness of existence is a pleasure.

The glittering sunshine, the soft rustling of the newly-come leaves stirred into motion by a passing breath, fills one with delight; and the hum of insects, and the song of birds chimes in, almost as an expression of one's own feeling.

In a life with a good many distractions, this feeling (almost a religious one) has no scope—action impedes thought; and in a life full of excitement, who pauses to analyse their pleasure!

Yes! what has been left unsaid about spring! It has been held up to admiration in lofty words, and measured and sonorous verse prosed about; made the scapegoat of aspiring poets (?) in the corners of many magazines, and ill-used over and over again by those whose poetical aspirations are undoubtedly great, but whose talent for versification is unfortunately small!

It is a hackneyed subject, and if I were going to write about " Vernal Spring " or " Eternal Spring," everyone would do well to pass on to something a little more amusing.

But the spring I am thinking about is a very different thing. There is a spring of the heart that succeeds *almost* every winter there, that revives it, and makes it young again, giving renewed love of life, fresh capacity for enjoyment.

It is the reaction of health (and all health gives,) sickness, when the absence of pain, or even of discomfort, is a pleasure appreciated from moment to moment. This spring came now to Bertha.

After her long and lingering illness, subdued and softened by her sufferings, and her separation from her husband, she had imagined herself so completely altered, that she had no longer a sympathy for any pleasure.

Under the influence of her anxiety about her husband, and the weight of her own illness, she felt as if her natural state now was dulness, and low spirits—she cared little how she dressed, or how she looked.

It was with surprise, therefore, that, under the genial influence of a very sunshiny day, Bertha found her spirits rising, and the old sanguine feeling again befriending her.

The lights and shadows cast by the flickering leaves, the glints of sunlight streaming through the tender green of the beech boughs, and lighting up into threads of gold the fair curls of her children, the merry and impertinent chirp of the saucy sparrows, all were noted and appreciated.

She was expecting Frank now daily, and, on such a day as I have described, was sitting with her work under the trees, when she saw Mr. Doall approaching her.

"Don't move, don't move," he said, as Bertha moved towards him, as if he were an emperor graciously permitting his subject to sit before him, and was kindly anxious to waive ceremony.

Bertha murmured some greeting in her usual quiet manner, and went on with her work.

Mr. Doall was evidently not quite himself; he fidgeted, and was more pompous and fussy than usual; and then to Bertha's extreme surprise, he said, in a tone of great solemnity—

"Mrs. Herbert, I believe you did not hear from your husband a few days ago, when you expected a letter?"

Bertha's heart sank within her, a cold, chill feeling, a foreboding of evil, came over her. She only bowed—words failed her!

"I have no bad news," hastily exclaimed Mr. Doall, in a great fright; "and for my sake don't faint, Mrs. Herbert; I have not a notion what to do with a fainting lady—none of *my* family ever did such a thing in their lives!"

"What is it?" said Bertha, trying to compose herself.

"The most good-natured actions are sometimes frustrated," said the Dollington rector, waving his hands after a fashion peculiarly his own, "by human fallibility." "Four days ago, Mrs. Herbert," he continued, after pausing vainly for the applause to which his family had so accustomed him on every occasion—"four days ago I was on my way to the clerical meeting, where my presence was particularly required, when I thought (one of those sudden impulses, I suppose, the origin of which is for some good reason withheld from us) of going to the post-office, and amongst other things I inquired of that excellent person,

Mrs. Black, the post-mistress, if she had any letters for you."

Bertha could not conceive what all this was to end in.

" Now, Mrs. Herbert, it is a very peculiar circumstance; please, if you have not already noticed it, look at my great coat."

Bertha looked at it, wondering more and more; the great coat was black, or rather *had been* black, and was now brownish, oldish, and, like the wearer, had a tendency to general shabbiness.

" There was a letter for you, Mrs. Herbert," continued Mr. Doall, " and in order that you might receive it sooner, I undertook to bring it to you. Unfortunately, but quite naturally, I forgot all about it till to-day. I'll explain it to you immediately; it was the most natural thing in the world. At the cross roads—you know the cross roads, Mrs. Herbert, at the top of the hill leading to the right side of the village, there

—I met a gentleman, an old college friend, and we fell into conversation. We went to our meeting together, and then I came home, and my coat, with the letter in the right-hand pocket, was put away. It was warm, if you recollect, the day before yesterday, very warm—too warm for this great coat—and yesterday I did not go out. To-day I hesitated, but my sister Betsy persuaded me, as I was to be out late to-night, to put it on. I put my hands into the pockets, and to my astonishment *there* was the letter! A very extraordinary thing, but you quite understand it could not possibly have been helped."

"Suppose you give it to me now," said Bertha, not a little amused by this specimen of Mr. Doall's usual manner, and expecting a common-place epistle, but her feelings can be imagined when she recognised the long-expected foreign letter, in her husband's handwriting.

Almost snatching it out of Mr. Doall's

hands, she astonished him by racing towards the house at full speed, leaving him without a word.

"God bless me!" he ejaculated, breathless with surprise. "What a very extraordinary person. Dr. Flapping said she was very excitable, and so she is. I never saw such an excitable person in all my life. I had not half finished what I had to say. Excitable, I should think so!" And, the rectorial dignity a little hurt by so sudden an exit, he wended his way home to discuss with his sisters Mrs. Herbert's "rapid action."

Had Bertha remained she would probably have surprised him still more; her indignation knew no bounds; how she had longed for this letter, congratulating her on baby's safe arrival, and fixing the day of his departure from Shanghae.

The contents of this delayed document soon absorbed her attention. It contained a long account of his journey, and its results; congratulated her and himself more upon her safety, and dwelt at length on the importance of taking care of herself. After telling her that he was waiting to see some one who had not yet arrived, a postscript was hastily added, saying he sent the letter in case of accident, but that he had just completed his business, and by the advice of the doctor there, whom he had been forced to consult, he was leaving for England then, and might be at home before, or as soon as, his letter.

And the letter was three days old! Any moment might bring him to her side. She started up, and full of pleasurable excitement, hastily gave orders, and commenced preparations for his arrival, breaking off every now and then to read over and over again the precious letter which Mr. Doall's kindly-*intentioned* action had so long delayed.

All at once, on approaching the window, she saw to her amazement and annoyance that again the portly form of the rector was standing confronting her.

"Excuse me, Mrs. Herbert," he said, "but my sister, Betsy, was anxious to know if you had had any news, as you seemed in such a state; if you wished it she would come down and talk it over with you."

"Oh! not on any account!" exclaimed Bertha, hastily. "Yes, I *have* had news—Mr. Doall, I am sorry to seem rude, but I am *very* busy. Mr. Herbert may arrive at any moment!"

"May I ask if that was contained in the letter I brought you this afternoon?" inquired Mr. Doall.

"Of course it was," said Bertha. "I have had no other. Goodbye."

"Goodbye, Mrs. Herbert. Good evening I ought to say," and drawing near her, he continued—"all things are ordered for the best. My meeting my friend at the cross roads, and all that, has been the luckiest thing imaginable, after all."

"What in the world do you mean?" asked Bertha, with visible impatience.

"Why, you see, Mrs. Herbert, my having had that letter in my great-coat pocket has been the best thing that could have happened. If three days ago you had been expecting your husband every moment, and, excuse me, you had been in such a state of excitement, it would have been very bad for you; so though, as I explained to you, I could not help it, and acted with the best possible intentions, you see, it is all right in the end, and quite does away with any little feeling of regret I had about the delay! *I* consider it a very extraordinary circumstance—almost, one may say, providential."

Bertha could not resist it; this complacent way of looking at his carelessness, was so completely part of the man's character, that she gave way to a fit of laughter; and after gazing at her for a moment with a grave doubt as to her sanity, Mr. Doall retreated; his sentiments on the subject of her excitability considerably increased.

CHAPTER XXIV.

"HOME! SWEET HOME!"

The lengthening shadows warned Bertha to bring in her children, and she sent them to bed—longing for perfect rest, perfect quiet, that she might realize her hope of soon, very soon, seeing her husband.

Too restless to remain in-doors, she walked down to the little gate that divided the small garden and grounds surrounding the cottage from the road, and leaned against it, listening, as only those listen who both hope and expect.

The air was still and calm; the drowsy bees were all wending homewards, tired with their busy day; the rooks were cawing their appreciation of a fine evening, as they settled down on their favourite trees; the small trotting sound of the tired children, taken home from play by their respective mothers; the clumsy tramping of the farm-horses going to water at the village pond, were the familiar sounds that alone broke the stillness for a time. Then—yes! at last, the quick and unmistakeable sound of a carriage and horses became evident. Faster and faster it drew near, and in a moment Bertha was clasped in her husband's arms!

When the first joys of meeting had found vent in happy tears—when the children, above all, baby, had been shown and admired, Bertha noticed with delight how well her husband was looking.

Bronzed with his sea voyage, but bright and cheerful, it was not only the pleasure of returning that gave him such an air of content. Bertha felt that his spirits were good, and that he had good news to tell. He was, however, not able to say so much about his wife. She looked still too delicate; and, though always slight, she now had a shadowy look about her that made him rejoice he was again · at home to take care of her.

How much they had to tell—how much to hear! Frank knew by his wife's account how keenly she had felt his absence; but she amused him by the way in which the Doall family were touched upon. Naturally enough, he was extremely indignant about the letter, and convulsed over the rector's self-satisfaction in the end. Bertha made light of her illness, except as regarded Miss Thurston's care of her; and these topics discussed during dinner, they found themselves afterwards, with full and thankful hearts, ready to talk over future plans; and Bertha was longing to hear *all* the particulars of her husband's journey.

Having satisfied her as far as he was able to do so, he went on to tell her of his exertions at Shanghae. He had inspected accounts, and examined witnesses, and had spared no trouble, till he was able to throw some light upon all the transactions, and send home valuable information. The delightful climax was, a cheque for a hundred pounds, presented to him by Mr. Carter, on behalf of the firm, who had also been very liberal as regarded expenses.

Frank also had a great deal to tell her about his plans. An unexpected opening had occurred; but before entering into it all, he was anxious to hear from her if she had any dislike to going abroad.

"Abroad! certainly not."

Bertha liked a foreign life immensely; and then the economy of living there was much greater: not going there, and living *à l'Anglaise*, as she carefully explained to her husband, but living without English servants, who were certain to have English wants, and a thousand troublesome requirements.

"And about society?"

Bertha answered wisely. She could not

honestly say how, in the face of her recent experience, that "solitude and one beside" was what she craved for; but there was, perhaps, less necessity for a hermitage abroad than one at home.

In all characters like Bertha's, there is generally one noble quality—"truth." Bertha was not only truthful towards herself, but she was the same towards others, often a much more difficult thing.

She acknowledged to her husband, as she had before done to herself, how much she had mistaken her own character, and how completely she accepted with gratitude the discipline she felt had been exactly what she wanted. If her husband had been inclined, she was quite prepared to blame herself for everything that had happened; but Frank's mind was essentially just. He felt that his own impatience had helped to place them in their trying position, and that, like all trials, they may be turned into blessings by ourselves. At any rate, it had brought out the finer and higher parts of *his* character, and had softened instead of hardening both; it had also given to each a better appreciation of the other, and had taught them more about their mutual affection than they could possibly have learnt any other way.

Bertha questioned him about his illness, and found it had been more severe than he had allowed at first. His doctor had insisted upon his hurrying home, and the journey had done him great good, and had brought about the expectations and hopes that he now began to acquaint Bertha with; but they were of such great importance, and opened up the prospect of such a complete change, that it was quite impossible to decide hurriedly, and without due reflection. No; if they had erred in making plans for themselves before, they had learnt patience now, and were determined to weigh their present prospects well, and give due consideration to every side of the question.

CHAPTER XXV.

M. LE COMPTE VON PEFFERSTEIN.

On board the steamer at Shanghai, where Frank—a sick and melancholy man—had taken his passage for the homeward journey, there was a passenger—a bustling, quick-eyed, active little man—whose conversation was made up of scraps and fragments of so many different languages that Frank, who could not help watching him with great amusement, could not conceive what nation had the honour of claiming him as a son.

His name was easily enough discovered. M. le Comte von Pefferstein was marked in full on so many portmanteaux, boxes, bags, and tin cases, and floated, inscribed on limp French cardboard, from such a quantity of parcels, that *it* was evident enough. But M. le Comte himself seldom began and ended a sentence in one language, and Frank could not make out to what country he belonged. He spoke English a little (so he said)—and it was a *very* little—and he spoke French like a German—that is to say, very ill indeed; but he evidently did not, could not, or would not, speak German altogether, even to one or two Germans on board.

After surveying him *à la manière Anglaise* for a day or two, the acquaintance was made by accident.

Frank's long legs stretched themselves out all their lazy length across a promenade which the little man was taking in front of him, and, with his eyes half closed, he was musing on things far enough removed from his present quarters. The little man, whose eyes were employed in surveying Frank's pale face and dejected countenance, and who was not in the least thinking of his legs, stumbled over them. Mutual apologies necessarily followed, and the acquaintance thus began flourished, all the better that Frank, ill and weak, was not in the full possession of the insular stiffness.

M. von Pefferstein was one of those happy beings who flatter themselves that all they do, say, and think is a matter of the utmost importance to all the rest of the world.

However recent the acquaintance, they lay hold of the smallest civility as an encouragement; a smile, however feeble, is construed into an amount of sympathy that justifies on the spot the most lengthy narration of facts relating solely to *self*, minute particulars, and trivial anecdotes, set forth in inflated language, and all turning to the same interesting centre-piece of attraction.

In spite, however, of all the egotism,

possessed by M. von Pefferstein in no ordinary degree, there was so much genuine kind-heartedness in the little man, and he was so thoroughly gentleman-like, that Frank liked him, and they became constant companions.

At the very beginning of their acquaintance Frank was told his whole history, that of his parents and grandparents, and a good many anecdotes of all his collateral relations. His ancestors were disposed of in a breath; and certainly, if an erratic life entitled a man to be communicative, M. von Pefferstein had that excuse.

Brought up at some old château near the Hartz Mountains, as a companion to a distant relation, a certain Prince Sauerlich, he found himself at the death of his father in possession of a château, in ruins, and its pleasure-grounds, *pour tout potage*. The whole of the rest of the property had been by degrees absorbed in the Sauerlich estate.

The prince (who, by his account, had

been fond of hunting and of nothing else) had insisted upon his remaining with him, and for three or four years he had remained there, tolerably satisfied with his position.

A change was brought about by the sudden death of his highness, who bequeathed a small independent fortune to his friend, and appointed him joint guardian with the mother over his little son.

The Prince von Sauerlich had married very much beneath him—*that* M. von Pefferstein admitted—but the lady, the daughter of a Dutch merchant, had not only had a good round sum of money, but expectations! She had two uncles who were merchants in India and China, and who were so properly grateful to their niece for giving them as a nephew a real live prince, that they had expressed their intention of testifying their gratitude in a most satisfactory way, by making her son principal heir to the fortunes for which they had broiled and toiled for so many years.

One of these considerate uncles died, and the princess, who was of rather a fussy disposition, was so perfectly convinced that she should lose thousands unless some one devoted to her son's interests was on the spot to assert his rights, that she became eloquent, and M. von Pefferstein, nothing loath, undertook the journey, armed with every imaginable credential.

Why, after accomplishing his mission with tolerable success, he should have gone to Japan, and was now going to England, he did not say; but he openly regretted that he had not seen more of the world, and informed Frank that when one more object was achieved he intended to indulge in the love of travel, which was his great passion.

With all the frankness and absence of reserve that he showed in relating all this to Frank, it was evident to the latter that there was something he held back; indeed, in the history of his life Frank found nothing to account for the smattering of English he used so frequently, and that was not always very refined.

Two or three days, however, before they landed in England it was evident that he must have a confidant as a safety valve. He was bursting with some important intelligence.

Inviting Frank to a private conference with an air of the deepest mystery, he told him that he was going to place great confidence in him, and under the seal of secrecy he told him the following facts:—

"Some years before the death of the late Prince von Sauerlich some mines had been discovered, which were supposed to be very valuable. If they were valuable, they were very badly managed, for they did not then pay their own expenses. At last M. von Pefferstein, who had read a great deal about the mines in Cornwall and the Cornish miners, had persuaded his friend to import a number of them to Germany to develop the resources of those at Sauerlich.

Naturally those that went over were the very roughest specimens of their class; and year after year there had been nothing but trouble and perpetual riots. Just before leaving home M. von Pefferstein had persuaded the princess to engage an English gentleman, accustomed to deal with these men, to go to Sauerlich, inspect the mines, and put things on a more satisfactory footing. If, by his report, the mines were valuable, they would continue working them; if he condemned them they would give up the prospect of making anything by them.

This gentleman had been there, and his report was so much more satisfactory than even the sanguine hopes of M. von Pefferstein had led him to believe, that the little man was in terror lest some English capitalist should hear of them, and come down upon them before he had had time to raise the sum necessary to carry out Mr. Tredgar's plans.

He was now on his way to London to meet Mr. Tredgar and arrange some matters with him, and he told Frank that he would feel much indebted to him if he would give him the address of an honest man of business, as that was essential to his success.

Frank was glad to have the opportunity of naming Mr. Carter, to whose house he was himself going, and the little count, who did not know a soul in London, was charmed, and said so with his usual volubility. They parted with mutual assurances of regard, and the prospect of meeting again speedily was a source of satisfaction to both.

CHAPTER XXVI.

FRANK HERBERT BECOMES SANGUINE.

It was satisfactory to Frank, after two hours of close business with Mr. Carter and the merchants on whose behalf he had gone to China, to find that his labours there were not considered in vain; on the contrary, he received the warmest thanks for the clear statements he had brought home, and over and above the expenses of his journey the Messrs. Rhind presented him with a cheque for one hundred pounds.

He had hardly had time after this to explain to Mr. Carter, in as concise a manner as possible, the business of the little count, when that individual was ushered in. After introducing the two gentlemen, Frank went upstairs to put his things together, intending to leave by an afternoon train and return home.

He had nearly completed his arrangements, when Mr. Carter knocked and entered.

"Your lively little friend is still downstairs," said he, "and wishes to speak one word to you before you go."

"I wish he would choose some other time," said Frank. "I shall miss my train and lose another day."

"You had better see him," said Mr. Carter; "he really has something to say to you."

Frank shrugged his shoulders, and ran downstairs. M. von Pefferstein was trotting up and down the room in a state of considerable excitement. He rushed up to Frank, and seizing him by both hands, exclaimed—

"Oh! my friend, you go?—say you go!" looking at him with imploring eyes.

Frank was most naturally utterly bewildered.

"Go!" he said. "Yes, I am going home," and as he gently shook off his friend he added, "that is, if you do not make me late for the train."

M. von Pefferstein began so incoherent an explanation, that Frank looked to Mr. Carter for assistance, and that gentleman persuaded the count to let him be spokesman.

It seemed that among Mr. Tredgar's suggestions about the mine was one to the effect that an English superintendent should be appointed at a salary of about four hundred pounds a year, and a house, and that he should have as his immediate subordinate an English overseer, with liberal pay. As a matter of precaution the superintendent was to have a surety, and thus the miners would have their own countrymen to deal with, and one great element of warfare would be avoided without risking anything.

When Mr. Tredgar had suggested this, he owned that it would be very difficult to get any one to accept the position of superintendent, who knew anything of mines, but he thought that if the overseer was a practical man and one to be trusted, it did not much signify. A clever man would soon learn enough, and he was required more to act as paymaster, referee, &c., than anything else.

When Mr. Tredgar spoke, it immediately occurred to Mr. Carter, that this post was one which would suit Mr. Herbert in many ways, and after preliminary details had been settled, and Mr. Tredgar had left, he asked M. von Pefferstein if Frank would not suit him in every way.

The delight of that gentleman at such a proposition was so unbounded, that Mr. Carter had to remind him of the possibility of Frank's refusal.

"Ask him now!" was all the count's answer to this; and having represented that

Frank could not be expected to give an immediate answer to so sudden a proposition, Mr. Carter had gone to fetch him.

All Frank could say was that he must take time to consider this new opening, and he must also consult his wife.

The Count was nearly inconsolable. His immediate intention was of proceeding to "Madame Herbert," where he should use every argument to overcome her prejudices, should she have any; and he was only prevented from carrying out this intention by being reminded by Mr. Carter that he had positively engaged himself to Mr. Tredgar that evening to dinner, and was to accompany him to Cornwall on the next day, for a week.

"At the end of that week," Mr. Carter said, "Mr. Herbert will let you know if he accepts the post you offer him; and as he is anxious to be off, we will detain him no longer."

Frank Herbert most gratefully availed

himself of this opening to escape, and hastily and warmly thanking Mr. Carter for all his kindness, he hurried off, M. von Pefferstein following him to the door, and reminding him, if "Madame" proved obdurate *he* was ready to go down at a moment's notice.

CHAPTER XXVII.

ANOTHER MOVE.

WHEN Frank and his wife came to consider all the advantages that the offered situation had, it is almost needless to say that they made up their minds to accept it.

Bertha had been abroad a good deal, and though she knew that going abroad to live in an out of the way part of the world, with arrangements enforced by a very tiny income, was widely different from going there with almost a retinue of servants and all the prestige consequent on being the only daughter of a man who, though not actually rich, always lived as if he were, she liked the idea, and had passed the town close to Sauerlich several times.

The advantages the plan held out were very many, putting aside the great consideration of an occupation for her husband, and the salary; so, long before the week was over, they decided upon accepting it, and Frank made M. von Pefferstein "the happiest person in the world" by writing and saying so.

It is difficult to describe the hopefulness and thankfulness of the Herberts under their present prospects. Bertha certainly longed to be able in some way to restore to Miss Thurston what she had lost; she wished also she could see something of the Haughtons; but apart from these wishes, she felt happier and more contented than she could express.

True, her various schemes had died a natural death. She had written nothing; her historical romance would never astonish the world; her opera had floated entirely away, but she was too practically busy now to do more than sometimes laugh at her own vivid imagination, and she did not even intend to write those practical sermons for which she had once imagined she had a special and particular talent.

As far as Frank was concerned he wanted nothing now but to see Bertha herself a little stronger. She was very far from strong, and though her complexion was a little embrowned by the sun, she looked anything but fitted for any more "roughing."

He remembered with a feeling of uneasiness that her mother had died while very young, and though his misgivings took no definite shape, they were sufficiently present to sober his spirits a little, and to prevent his entering with such a full tide of happiness into the future as Bertha did.

He was also essentially English, and was not at all one of those men intended for a citizen of the world. He knew French only as in those days public-school boys did, and he hated the language, and the few foreigners who formed the limit of his experiences. Certainly, Sauerlich was not in France, but that only made things worse. Of course, if the French were so unlike his ideas of what was nice, what must those unhappy people be still further from this land of liberty and enlightenment!

After a brisk correspondence carried on with Mr. Carter and Mr. Tredgar, and a few epistles from M. von Pefferstein himself, it was arranged that Mr. Herbert should go down as soon as he could to Cornwall, to be the visitor of Mr. Tredgar for a little time, and to learn a few things likely to be of special importance to him in future.

Bertha and the children were to go to London for two or three weeks. She longed to see some of her relations again, and Frank felt that perhaps this would be the best thing possible for her.

Before leaving, they had of course to say good-bye to the Doall family.

Bertha had lost considerably in their

good opinion on farther acquaintance. Nothing annoyed them so much as the constant reserved civility which left them nothing to complain of, and yet kept them all at so great a distance. They positively knew no more of her than the first day they met; and, accustomed to a general intimacy with the people they knew, they disliked being upon this footing with their nearest neighbour. They had consoled themselves generally by expressing their opinion of her in a rather patronizing way —" poor thing," and " poor young thing" being the usual term; but since Mr. Herbert's return, and the adventure of the letter, they had felt affronted, and mingled a little abuse of their neighbour's eccentricity and " excitablity" with their usual manner of mentioning her.

Miss Betsy, too, had to forgive the little episode in her dealings with Miss Thurston. *That* conversation, and the consciousness of having placed herself in an absurd position, were still sore recollections. Like some people with very limited interests, all the Doalls adopted as their own the few to whom they extended their protection. They considered Mrs. Herbert's non-appreciation (to use the mildest term) of Dr. Flapping as almost a personal insult. They considered him so clever, that they thought her saying he was the very reverse was a reflection upon their judgment, and resented it with all the bitterness of which they were capable.

When the Herberts approached the rectory, they found the place exactly as on their first visit, with the exception of everything looking still more desolate and deserted. Bricks and a few stones were still lying about just as before, but time had clothed them here and there, although scantily, with the moss that creeps over damp stones, and the planks were split up and warped with constant exposure to rain and sun alternately.

They were ushered into the same room as before by a girl like "Mary," but who emerged from a dark passage wiping the soapsuds from her arms; and the room had the same odour of wine and onions.

The inmates, however, advanced towards the Herberts with an air of grandeur that sat amusingly upon them, and there was a visible stiffness.

"Going away!" "Very extraordinary!" The fact was commented on in various keys.

Miss Jane, the meekest of the family, and the one who suffered most when Miss Betsy was "grand," was sincerely sorry for Bertha, who must, she thought, be utterly crushed by the excessive severity of her sister's manner.

Mr. Doall contented himself by giving them a great deal of good advice. He had never been abroad himself; but that did not matter. He had read and had formed theories, and he enlarged upon his views till the inevitable "Good-by" was over—even then, he sent his sonorous voice after them, reminding them of his predictions.

Miss Betsy's most severe remark was not much felt by Bertha. *Her* heart was dancing with happiness, and the Doall family heard with astonishment the ringing laughter that floated on the air as husband and wife retraced their homeward steps.

The next morning witnessed their departure. Frank took Bertha to London, established her there with the children, and left for Cornwall without waiting to see anyone.

CHAPTER XXVIII.

BERTHA RENEWS ACQUAINTANCE WITH SOME OF HER RELATIONS AND FRIENDS.

LONDON is an enchanting place for a few months "in the season," when all the world is there.

To a young and happy girl, with a good many advantages and a definite position, it is delightful.

Conscious of being perfectly dressed, and whirled along in an easy barouche, life is pleasant to her.

It is not *then* that worldly cares press upon her mind; the world, as yet, has not disappointed her; she imbibes the honey, and ignores the possibility of a sting.

The faithlessness of friends—the insincerity, the hollowness which distinguish the world, according to the tenets of those embittered beings who inveigh against fashion and society, because society and fashion have passed them by, may possibly exist, but not for her.

She has probably fresh and very unworldly sentiments; and, as a rule, a young girl in her first season is not the worldling some people endeavour to depict her. If she thinks of love or matrimony, in nine cases out of ten she will take the natural and romantic view of it. The imaginary being is to possess the most exquisite figure —a head where talent and beauty are combined; he is to have a deep low voice, and be stern and rather severe at the proper moment—be a member of Parliament, as a matter of course, and make speeches that take every one by surprise, from their extraordinary combination of gigantic intellect, deep thought, and great facility of expression: of pounds, shillings and pence, she does not think at all, in all probability.

In the mean time she is petted and fêted to her heart's content; and the chances are, that she feels perfectly good-humoured, and looks something like the angelic being infatuated young men proclaim her.

It is also pleasant to be mounted to perfection—conscious of doing justice to the perfect fit of Woolmerhausen's last new habit—the riding hat, saved from being masculine by a fairy veil that tends to embellish—the tiny hands, well guarded, controlling the movements of an apparently spirited steed, in Rotten Row—recognising one friend, chatting to another, and arranging diplomatically the various engagements of the evening, with a view (not often successful) of pleasing yourself and satisfying your chaperone at the same time—discussing last night's opera, or the coming *soirée dansante*, when you expect to meet all your favourite partners. . . . It is certainly very pleasant!

Bertha had engaged in rather more than

her share of all this. Not handsome or (what is more dangerous) attractive enough to create a sensation of fear in the minds of mothers of eldest sons, she was handsome enough to be accounted a beauty by *very* young men, and to be pronounced a distinguished-looking girl by their seniors. Also, the magical word "money!" was whispered about in connexion with her name; and it was only natural that the ten thousand pounds she was really entitled to became five times that sum when quoted by the world.

She was also very popular among girls of her own standing. They instinctively recognised in her a want of worldliness that might have clashed with their own pet plans. She never made mischief between them and their favourite partners; she never told fibs, and she never monopolized a friend's admirer (however fascinating he might be), unless that friend was well out of the way.

Bertha also, from being motherless, and peculiarly frank in her manner, had (as is usual) twice the admiration and interest *expressed* than it would be safe to show to a young lady with a vigilant mother, who might possibly take those warm expressions of admiration for something more than is actually intended. Most men find out soon enough what *style* of compliment takes best with a girl; and though Bertha had (to do her justice) a very small share of personal vanity, she liked to hear herself "appreciated," as far as her talents and accomplishments were concerned.

Lady Haughton's habits of indolence also gave Bertha prestige. Thanks to *them*, she was generally the last to appear at a ball, when she came in, looking fresh and radiant —in brilliant contrast to those girls whose roses and dresses had faded in a few hours' encounter of heat and crush; and she went away so early, that if people wished to dance with her or talk to her, they knew they must make the most of the present opportunity; so she had as much on her hands as she could manage during the time she stayed.

Bertha's singing was another strong point in her favour. She was far too indifferent to the remarks some people are sure to make about the singing of every amateur, to care if the people talked or not. She sang brilliantly; and the subdued buzz of conversation never put her out at all; and this talent in London is as invaluable as it is rare.

From all this, it will be seen that all her London experiences had been very pleasant ones, and that the change in her present circumstances was likely to be doubly felt.

Guided by the remembrance of visits paid to friends in the dim and dirty lodgings that combined extravagance in price with everything most distasteful to her *in* London, Bertha had obtained lodgings near Kensington. Very small they certainly were, but they were clean, and not at all dear. When she found herself established there, she wrote to most of her relations, and told them where she was to be found, also mentioning that her husband was not with her at the moment, that he had got an appointment abroad, and that they were then on their way there. Having taken this step, she busied herself in providing a few tidy things to set her pretty children off to better advantage, and awaited the result of her communications with a feeling of excitement natural from the retired life she had led for so long a time.

CHAPTER XXIX.

LADY CECIL.

"My dear Bertha!" exclaimed her father's sister, Lady Cecil, when, in compliance with that lady's request, Bertha arrived in Grosvenor-street. "I am delighted to see you again—quite delighted! I thought you had retired from civilized life altogether. Dear me, my dear, how very, *very* much you are altered. It is such a pity, living entirely in the country, and getting so utterly regardless of your complexion. You are terribly freckled, my dear child—absolutely sunburnt!"

"I dare say I am," said Bertha, very composedly; "but it really does not much signify."

"Does not much signify, my dear!" exclaimed Lady Cecil, horror-stricken. "My dear, I do trust you have not imbibed such very sad—such very republican ideas. I consider that taking care of one's personal appearance is a social duty!"

"What I meant," said Bertha, "was, that as I was not going out anywhere, it did not matter very much what state my complexion was in."

"I am not *quite* sure," continued her aunt, "that it is not the effect of that *excessively* unbecoming bonnet you have on. Do you mind taking it off?"

"Oh, my dear, how horribly ill your hair is done, to be sure! That's *the* most trying way of doing the hair, and nobody wears it that way now. It's quite antique. Have you a maid?"

"No," said Bertha, shortly.

"Ah! my dear," said Lady Cecil, sighing deeply and shaking her head, "I never liked to say so by letter, because your husband might have seen it. I've no doubt he's very charming, and all that, but it was a sad mistake that marriage of yours. You are not in the least fitted for that life. I always said and felt what a mistake you made, and if you had only had a little patience you might have made a very good marriage indeed. I am sure you always had plenty of admiration. If you had chosen differently——"

"I never could have had a more generous, a more devoted husband!" cried Bertha, warmly.

"Of course, he's devoted to you, my dear," returned her aunt, coolly; "he has every reason to be. Look at all the sacrifices you have made for his sake."

"Sacrifices! Oh! Aunt Cecil, do you not know," exclaimed Bertha, "it was not his fault at all? You forget it was my miserable money that was lost; it was Uncle Germayne that was to blame."

"I do not forget at all," said Lady Cecil,

calmly; "but if you had married a man with even *some* money, as you ought to have done, your fortune might have disappeared without your missing it in the least. However, it's done now, and we must make the best of it. I am very glad to hear that he has got an appointment. What is it?"

Without pausing for an answer, she went on—"I don't take any credit to myself, my dear, but the other night, when I met Mr. Higginson, of the Shuffling-office, I could not lose so good an opportunity of putting in a word, and I told him that you had made a most wretched marriage, and were miserably poor——"

"Thank you!" said Bertha, sarcastically.

"You need not thank me, my dear," said her aunt; "I am sure I will always gladly do any little good-natured thing in my power for you. Well, I told Mr. Higginson that if there *was* any little thing in his power, your husband would be so very glad of it; and I added, my dear, that I believed he was perfectly well-educated, and I was sure he could spell (which is *the* thing, I fancy)—not that I had ever seen his letters, but I was quite sure, my dear Bertha, you never would marry a man who couldn't. Well, my dear, he *said* nothing—these public men are so cautious, you know— but I felt sure he took it all in, and *very* likely it led to this appointment."

Bertha felt how useless it was to quarrel with anyone so perfectly satisfied with her own views of everything; she merely said, "This appointment is abroad, Aunt Cecil —not in England."

"Abroad! how very lucky! something in the Colonies?" said Lady Cecil, cheerfully. "Much nicer for you! After all, London would have been very expensive, and the Colonies are all very cheap, and any sort of dress does there; indeed, I know as a fact that in some places the people of the country wear no clothes at all!"

"I do not suppose that fashion would

influence *us* much," said Bertha, laughing; "but this is not a colonial appointment; it is to superintend some valuable mines in Germany. When I say superintend, it is not exactly that, for Frank will have an English overseer under him, but my husband will have all the responsible part; all the money will go through his hands."

Lady Cecil's face lengthened considerably. "You entirely misled me, my dear; you called it *an appointment*. Now, an appointment, all the world knows, means something belonging to Government. Superintendent over some mines! really, that does not sound much. I could not say in society, you know, if I am asked, who you married. I could not say my niece is married to a superintendent of mines! That would *never* do!"

"The mines belong to the Prince of Sauerlich," said Bertha; "and it does not signify what the world says; the great point is a very fair salary, with a house and garden, and it will give Frank something to do."

"But, my dear, are you quite sure Prince what's-his-name is a real prince. My dear Bertha, *be* cautious. There was that horrid man who stole my sister-in-law's spoons, and did all sorts of dreadful things, and he called himself Prince or Count something."

"We know this man is a real Prince," said Bertha. "Perhaps we may come back quite rich," she added, gaily.

"Oh! my dear child, whatever you do, don't allow your husband to speculate; railways are dreadful things. I lost one hundred pounds some years ago in a horrible company, I hardly knew what I took shares in."

"We shall have nothing to do with railways," said Bertha.

"Well, my dear, railways or mines, it is all the same thing exactly," said Lady Cecil; "it is all speculation; and speculation, my dear Bertha, is a very terrible thing. I wish you could persuade your husband to leave it off, and give this place up. We can so easily find something else for him to do. People, of course, will talk about it so much," she added, musingly.

"It does not seem to me that 'something to do *is* so easily found," said Bertha; "and as we are not in the way of hearing what people say, why should we care?"

"Very selfish, indeed, my dear," said Lady Cecil; "if you do not care for yourself, you might have some feeling for your relations. People will say *we* might have come forward, and all sorts of things. I am sorry to say your ideas have become very provincial; no, not provincial, but democratic; just like the French when they killed their king and queen. It is quite shocking, my dear; you should try and keep up your tone of mind, and not give way to those feelings. Not care what people say! Why, the world would quite come to an end if we all thought in that way!"

Bertha tried to talk of other things, but found that she and her aunt had so little in common, that she soon rose to say good-by.

Lady Cecil begged her to remember that she would always be happy to see her; but allowed her to depart without recollecting that she had to find her way to Kensington either on foot, or in a cab, which latter alternative she was obliged to take, and returned to her little lodging vexed with her aunt, and completely tired out. What she could least of all forgive was the fact, that Lady Cecil had not once asked for her children!

CHAPTER XXX.

COUSINS.

When Bertha reached home she found two little notes awaiting her; the offspring of the afternoon post—both were invitations.

One was an enthusiastic effusion from a cousin of her own age, who was still unmarried.

She said she was enchanted to hear that Bertha was actually in London, and that (as she and her sister had heaps of engagements) she wanted her to come to a severe tea in their own sitting-room next day; they were not going to appear at dinner, as they meant to enjoy themselves quietly preparatory to the opera, and an ensuing ball. The carriage should be sent for her early in the afternoon.

Bertha was pleased with the note, and the thoughtfulness about the carriage, and resolved to go.

Early in the afternoon, however, meant a little after five, and at that time she found herself once more whirling over the stones in a comfortable and pretty "turn-out."

Arrived in Grosvenor Square she was smuggled upstairs by her cousins' French maid, and she was greeted with the warmest embraces and exclamations of pleasure by the sisters.

Their raptures would, perhaps, have been more flattering had they not turned from her to Louise, who had a box of artificial flowers in her hand, and the exclamations of delight on her appearance with it —certainly equalled—if not surpassed in warmth the joy they had testified on Bertha's arrival.

"Louise! *Voyez donc!*" exclaimed Cynthia, in an ecstasy—"entirely my own idea. Swear Mrs. Styles to secrecy, and the effect *is perfect!*"

Louise, in voluble French, confirmed her praise.

Mary, the other sister, was evidently not so much pleased: when a dark and a fair sister choose to dress alike, occasional sacrifices of effect must ensue.

Cynthia, with a brunette complexion and jetty hair, affected gorgeous tints, and the wreath in question—French honeysuckle—exquisitely arranged, was very becoming to her.

Mary, who was more of a blonde and had a great deal of colour, felt that its tints did *not* set her off to the best advantage; and the sisters began to support their different opinions with no little warmth. Bertha's presence was utterly forgotten pending so momentous a question. Louise, appealed to by both, agreed with each in turn, and Bertha could not help admiring the tact with which she reconciled both sisters. She reminded Mary that, being some years younger than her sister, her freshness of complexion required less studying than Cynthia's; and just as the latter was on the verge of being offended, she turned towards her with a nod of intelligence, saying soothingly, "*Laissez, laissez donc! Mademoiselle, c'est fini.*"

The sisters at length dismissed her, and began to recount their gaieties, plans, hopes, and expectations, past, present, and to come.

"Where are you going to-night?" asked Bertha, "and what are you going to wear?"

"To Lady Hendley's," answered Cynthia, "after the opera. It has been so very difficult to decide what to put on, because the ball is to be *very* early, and mamma will not let us come home and change."

"I understand," said Bertha, "and of

course it will be a pity to sacrifice a very pretty dress. At Lady Hendley's, at least, if she still crowds those small rooms of hers, as she did in my day——"

"They are worse than ever," answered Mary; "it always costs us new skirts going there, and we have only just got new blue dresses to suit the new opera hangings. Blue is the only thing one looks decent in, with the present decorations there; so we do not wish to wear them, and altogether it has been so very difficult to decide," and Mary sighed deeply.

Bertha remembered well similar grievances, and sympathized accordingly.

"Mamma has been bored to death by people wanting her to get invitations to the Duchess of Branlingham's concert, because they know we are relations," said Cynthia.

"By-the-bye, Bertha, how many children have you got?"

"Two," answered Bertha. "A boy and a girl."

"Dear me! how funny," said Cynthia. "Only two? I thought you had half-a-dozen. I'm quite sure somebody told me so. My dear Bertha, where did you get those boots? They must have been made by the Laplanders? Are your children handsome, and can they talk and walk, and all that sort of thing? and do you like them, or do they bore you?"

"They are very like Frank," said Bertha. "and one can talk and—"

"Bertha, did you ever meet those gaping Crawford girls," interrupted Cynthia. "They wanted to get asked to the concert, and coolly wrote to mamma. Of course, she said she was giving nothing, and could ask for nothing. Wasn't it cool?"

"Very," said Bertha, laughing, "only I do not know who they are. I never heard of them before!"

"Daughters of some country baronet no one ever knew anything about till this year," said Mary. "There are such a number of them—very large, very overdressed, with high colours and high voices; they quite fill a room if they all appear together. They have a dreadful brother, with pink cheeks, curly hair . . . . and sloping shoulders."

"Poor man!" said Bertha, compassionately.

"Terrible man!" laughed Cynthia; "if you *only* heard him talk, with his eyes half shut, his head on one side, drawling out his notions of things, and talking of his fastidiousness, when he has been till lately a clerk in something or other—a bank or a brewery, or something of the kind."

"He ought to have more sense," said Bertha; "he probably will be well snubbed, and turn out better than you give him credit for."

"Don't be so dreadfully sensible," said Mary. "Snubbing! He is quite impervious to any snubbing. His sisters do nothing but admire him all day long, except when they are admiring themselves."

"He's not worth abusing," said Cynthia.

"Bertha, is it true you are going to the Caribbee Islands?"

"Or elsewhere," said Bertha, laughing. "Is that Aunt Cecil's last new idea?"

"She said *abroad*, and gave a very deep sigh, and pointed you out (of course you don't mind my telling you) as a warning to us, and the great folly of marrying upon nothing at all! Of course I concluded you were going to some dreadful place, and the Caribbee Islands came into my head."

"Put the Caribbee Islands out of it again and put Germany in," said Bertha.

"Oh! something in the diplomatic line," said Cynthia. "That sounds *very* nice!"

"It is not diplomatic," said Bertha; "but I think I must go and see your mother for a minute and then order the carriage. You will be late if you do not begin to dress; and I want to get home to the children;" and after a little desultory talk she rose to leave.

"Oh! the children!" exclaimed Cynthia,

laughing. "We heard you came out splendidly in the character of *mère de famille*, and that you walked about with one upon each arm, like the poor women with twins who always come to beg when the policemen are out of sight."

"Thanks for the comparison," said Bertha, very much amused, as she left the room to find her aunt.

Lady Vernon was "resting," her hair "dressed," all ready but her gown, as she explained to Bertha. She was kind, but not very cordial. She considered Bertha had been self-willed about her marriage, and did not think the example a very good one. Bertha submitted with a tolerable grace to the interminable cross-questioning, and gladly returned to her quiet lodgings at Kensington.

The interview had altogether been disappointing enough. It is quite true they asked a great many questions about her husband and the children, but they never gave her a chance of answering them. They were absorbed in their own amusements, or in grievances so small, in Bertha's eyes, that she could hardly forbear smiling.

Yes, she embraced her children all the more warmly on her return home, and she wrote a long and *very* affectionate letter to her husband, gratefully remembering that here, at least, she would meet with no disappointments; and she felt thankful that she had so much real and substantial comfort in her life—comfort that rendered her so completely independent of all the chills and indifference of the outer world.

Her boots might look like the cobbling of Laplanders; Frank did not think so; and if he did, he only honoured her the more for adapting herself to her circumstances. And if he was pleased, what in the world did it signify?

All the same, Bertha examined her boots that night, and owned they might be improved upon.

CHAPTER XXXI.

BERTHA SEES LONDON UNDER NEW AUSPICES.

Some weary days, and some very dreary ones, Bertha passed in the little Kensington lodging.

How dreary London can be, is only known to those who have experienced both phases of life there.

Some days Bertha saw no one and was apparently forgotten; at other times, a breakfast given in that direction would be seized upon as a good opportunity for paying a visit to "poor Bertha," when the street would be filled with carriages, and the footmen's knocks annihilated the nervous neighbours, and caused the door (thin of make, and out of all proportion with the aristocratic vigour of the salutation) to quiver and tremble underneath the infliction. The gaily dressed occupants fluttered up-stairs, fidgetted about, were afraid of being late in one or two minutes, and went off again. If they stayed, they were generally so completely occupied by their own interests that they asked fifty questions without waiting for any answer, and launched out into descriptions of people, places, and things — profusely interspersed with " of course you know "—something that Bertha had never heard.

Frank's letters were very cheering. He appeared in London only for one day, and hurried on to Sauerlich, eager to arrange for Bertha's comfort abroad, and urged on by her own anxiety to get away from London and its daily disappointments.

There is no doubt that, with the exception of a few, Bertha's relations did not trouble themselves much about her. Why should they? And there is also no doubt that the fact of their indifference made Bertha turn with increased affection to her husband and her home.

She was charmed, therefore, when his first letter arrived. He had had an interview with the princess, and described her as a jolly little woman, something in shape like a globular Dutch cheese—altogether kindly, and full of delight at the prospect of having an English lady so near her.

She had entered into the minutest particulars with the somewhat astonished Mr. Herbert, even enlarging upon the advantages to be derived from washing at home; but what was much more delightful to Frank, and that now sent Bertha's spirits up to a high pitch, she had asked if Madame Herbert would bring an English governess with her, to instruct her young son in that language. She left the selection entirely to Madame Herbert, because she was anxious that she should reside with them and give daily lessons to her son.

She had an attached German person, full of every virtue, but—a little jealous of strangers, whom she wished neither to part with nor offend.

Of course Miss Thurston occurred to Frank, and he mentioned her. The princess was convinced from the first that M. Herbert had only been born to rescue her out of every difficulty. Bertha was *perfectly* charmed; the prospect of having her dear old friend with her again was the only thing wanted to complete her felicity.

She wrote by that post—a much less eloquent letter would have done than the one she forwarded, in which she dwelt upon her husband's satisfaction and her own delight—for Miss Thurston was quite as pleased as Bertha—and the whole plan was settled without any delay. As soon as she had disposed of her house, &c., Miss

Thurston was to join Bertha in London, and they were to go abroad together. Bertha would willingly wait for her, and, indeed, she felt as if the silver lining to her cloud was showing already.

CHAPTER XXXII.

THE DUCHESS OF BRANLINGHAM.

Among the friends and acquaintances of Bertha's young-lady time in London was one whom she had almost entirely lost sight of in later days.

She had married some years before Bertha, and her life was quoted by all, except the envious, as the happiest that could possibly be. An heiress and an only child, she had never been in the very least spoiled, partly from the strong good sense of both father and mother, and partly from natural strength of character.

She was one of those people so large-hearted by nature, so frank and so generous, to whom everything small, mean, or narrow is an impossibility. Of course there is a good deal to be said about the effects of unchecked prosperity.

It is argued, and with some show of reason, that it is very easy to be generous about other people, and to make allowances for more or less prominent defects, when all goes well with oneself, and that nothing can be more natural than to excuse faults that cannot possibly affect you.

But the very fact of continued prosperity causes some natures to warp into carelessness and indifference. It is really difficult for a person whose experience of trials is simply and entirely through those of other people, to enter into them; and it is rare to find any one whose sympathy is quick enough to respond to the call made upon it, even by an intimate friend, and deep enough to enter into sorrows without betraying how little really they can realize them.

The character of some men fits them generally far more for real deep sympathy than that of women. A man's friendship for man, and sometimes for a woman, is of a much deeper, firmer, and more solid nature.

In the latter case, though so much nonsense is talked about it, there is the great charm of a perfect absence of jealousy, or what produces jealousy.

A woman, in a great many instances, is nominally "devoted" to a particular friend, but it does not grieve her to the soul if the shortcomings of that friend be noted by any one else. If she is sincere and good, *she* will not disparage her, nor even allow her to be disparaged; but she will, in her own mind, allow that there is a "good deal of truth" in whatever has been said.

If she is not very sincere or not very good, it will be very pleasant to her to endeavour to disturb her friend's too great equanimity by telling her (out of sheer kindness, of course,) what a mistake she has made on some one occasion, repeating with many apologies the unkind, unjust, or disparaging remarks which have probably been simply uttered by a time-serving person entirely to gratify *her*. Her friend is too comfortable, has too good an opinion of herself. She must show her friendship by putting her on her guard, and putting her on less good terms with herself.

The fact is that the old homely proverb, "Set a thief to catch a thief," applies very often to women's friendships. They are too quicksighted about each other's foibles, and judging others by themselves, credit their friends with just so much, and no more, of all they themselves possess in the way of disinterestedness, and a thousand other feminine virtues.

In all this the Duchess of Branlingham formed a very singular and happy exception. Married very young to a man of whom she was most passionately fond, the world had consoled itself for a marriage to which no one exception could be taken by reflecting upon the numberless mistakes the young duchess would make, forced so young into so prominent a position.

But the world witnessed no such mistakes. Single-hearted and straightforward, she intuitively avoided remark, and quietly assuming her place she reigned supreme, rejoicing evidently in the powers of an ample income because it conferred on others so much happiness and increased her own powers of making people happy.

To *her*, no ill-natured stories were carried and no one ventured to disparage any one. Her fair sweet face was only saddened by the effects of real sympathy, and she had the rare gift of really throwing herself into other people's interests. She really understood what sympathy was in its highest, widest, and deepest sense.

Dazzlingly fair, her movements were calm without nonchalance, and the blue eyes that enlivened her face reflected the noble spirit that ruled within. From her position she exercised a great influence, and how much she elevated the tone of all around her—how much the better most were for being brought into contact with her—she herself was the last person likely to know.

Those people less prosperous than herself she neither crushed by patronizing pity nor neglected; she could listen with real and not assumed interest to the disappointments of a mother in the married choice of a self-willed daughter, and sympathized with a girl in her first season deprived of some trifling pleasure. She could understand and forgive the ill-concealed bitterness of some person who had received an ill-deserved slight, and rejoice over an unexpected phase of good fortune in the life of another who was acquainted more with the sad than the bright side of things. She found something to like in everybody, perhaps because she insensibly drew out the best side of every one's character.

She was like a lovely flower, that yields

a fragrant odour whenever it is touched; and like the fragrance, spread far and wide.

The duchess had persuaded her husband to build her a lovely villa near Kensington, and there she usually received her friends. Her fêtes were celebrated far and near, while all the happy world invited there lingered under the bee-haunted chestnuts, felt rural for the moment, and wished itself out of town.

When Bertha fixed upon Kensington it was not without a hope of finding the duchess at Marley Lodge; she remembered her so well, that she felt certain if she was at home she would have a sympathizing friend near her; but the illness of one of the duke's relations had detained her, and it was not till Bertha had been some days at Kensington that she arrived there.

The morning after Bertha had received Miss Thurston's letter, she was preparing to go out with her children, when the panting maid-of-all-work rushed up stairs and announced a "lady."

It was the Duchess of Branlingham, with two of her dogs, who had walked down to see her.

Bertha thought she had not seen anything so lovely for a very long time; flushed a little with the cool morning air, her friend's beauty was a positively refreshing thing to her, peculiarly susceptible as she was to the influences of that charm which the duchess possessed.

With the tact peculiar to herself, Bertha's children were noticed and all the natural questions asked and answered without the faintest indication on her part of there being a change in Bertha's fortunes. Before she had been there many minutes, indeed, Bertha had entirely forgotten that she was at all in a position to be pitied.

CHAPTER XXXIII.

COMMON SENSE.

It is wonderful how easily and how soon everything that is false and not real, everything meretricious and that has no actual existence, that belongs simply to the imagination, melts and fades away before the honest, truthful, wholesome light let in upon it by such a person as the Duchess of Branlingham.

It is true that Bertha valued her husband's affection, and held firmly to her private conception of the share of happiness that was hers; Lady Cecil and Lady Vernon might say what they liked, others might insinuate what they pleased: Bertha piqued herself upon the stability of her sentiments and the justness of her views.

But it must be owned that the perpetual lamentations over Bertha's poverty, the incessant insinuations as to what *might* have been, and the brilliant prospects she had voluntarily resigned, all had their effect; and Bertha felt that she *had* resigned a great deal, and that in yielding herself so good-humouredly to a life of obscurity—in accepting a future so full of care—she had shown herself capable of great things; and she rose in her own estimation when she reflected how calmly all had been resigned. She was on the verge of erecting herself upon a little pinnacle, and admiring herself in the capacity of one of those heroines whose qualities were none the less that they were only recognised by a few, when the Duchess of Branlingham stepped in to the rescue.

Impossible, when so warmly congratulated upon the blessings she had, to make light of them; she could not, in the face of hearing herself talked of as fortunate in securing such an affection as Frank's and such an excellent husband, attempt to sigh over the one thing he wanted, "money," especially when the duchess took her at her word, and reminding her of her constant diatribes against worldly wealth, echoed her sentiments cordially, so far as it, and it alone, did not constitute happiness in the way some people fancied. As the duchess dwelt upon the advantages she possessed, one by one, Bertha began to see herself in a new light, and when she had confided the history of her money matters, she fancied that her husband and not herself was the most commiserated. How nobly he had borne the trial, by Bertha's own account! How many men would have constantly and untiringly harped upon such a theme to the destruction of all home happiness? Every word she said was felt by her friend. All the talk which Lady Cecil and others had poured into Bertha's half-willing ears was swept away, and she saw how nearly, in spite of her good resolutions, she was falling back into the old ungrateful habits of thought. It was a little humiliating, especially for one who considered herself to have such extremely well-grounded opinions.

The walks were long and constant under the chestnut trees, and did Bertha more good, by counteracting the evil that some of her other friends insensibly did her, than Bertha ever knew.

Frank's next letter was to the effect that he hoped she would now start immediately, as he had got everything ready, and only did not expatiate upon her new home because he was so afraid of raising her expectations too high. The house he thought charming, only it was too large—a novel experience in their married life. Miss Thurston arrived, and bidding farewell to all she could see in so short a time, Bertha and her friend, with the two little children, left England without a single regret.

CHAPTER XXXIV.

ABROAD.

It was on a broiling July day that Bertha, Miss Mary Thurston, and the two children arrived by the diligence at the little secluded village, where Frank met them.

Such a quaint little place! One long street, with tall and short houses jumbled together, a little canal running down one side of the street, and small trees planted at intervals in a formal way, and shorn of all excrescences in the shape of irregular boughs and branches that might have interfered with the German views of tidiness.

The lazy, lounging figures of a group of peasants, in their blouses and heavy wooden shoes, who had been doing nothing because the diligence had not come, and were doing nothing now because it had come, moved themselves into a slight semblance of activity as it rolled on.

Bertha's bright English face, as well as the look of the children, proclaimed them foreigners, and English—and they came a little forward, to see if this unexpected arrival was likely to be productive to them of exertion (which they hated), or of payment (which they loved).

"*You* must speak to them, Bertha," said Frank, when the first delights of meeting had a little subsided. "They are, without exception, the most dreadful people I ever saw. They all talk through their noses; and I cannot understand a single word they say."

Bertha, who had a strange feeling of being quite at home with them, turned and asked them if she could get a carriage to convey herself, her party, and luggage, to the town of Desseldringen.

"How far is it?" she inquired of her husband, as the united voices chorussed "Ya!"

"About three miles," he answered. "I walked down here; it is up-hill the whole way."

Bertha explained what she wanted to the men, who again chorussed, "So,—gut," and nodding their heads with a look of intelligence, they disappeared.

In a few minutes a wonderful looking machine was dragged forth, to which were harnessed three clumsy, thick-set, strong-looking horses, all abreast. By degrees, and with a great many guttural ejaculations, the luggage was piled upon the top; and finally, the party were installed inside, accompanied up the very steep hill by a few of the do-nothings.

The driver, with an amiable confidence in the steadiness of his horses and the hill, walked indifferently on a little paved footway by the side of the road, every now and then cracking his whip, and sometimes rushing up the steep bank in search of half-ripened nuts. Finding that he lost ground by this proceeding, he would actually run till he put himself again on a level with his horses—very red in the face, breathing loudly, and otherwise showing only too plainly that the heat of the day was *melting!*

The road wound round the side of a steep hill, and as the view opened beneath their feet an exclamation of delight and wonder burst from both Mary Thurston and Bertha.

At their feet stretched a valley indescribably beautiful, threaded by a broad and winding river.

As far as the eye could reach its silvery thread peeped out among wooded knolls. Here and there a little church spire pointed upwards from among a cluster of cottages. The ground, undulating and bathed in sunlight, was smiling with dotted cornfields, broken into and encroached upon by masses of wood and rich pastures, that gave to the picture the repose it wanted; while in the distance the jagged and massive outlines of some rugged hills broke the sky-line and framed the whole.

As they passed on, each turn of the road seemed to bring fresh beauties before their eyes. It was the evidence of God's power in its most lovely shape, and caused Bertha's heart to "sing for joy."

At the entrance of Desseldringen stood their future home; and as the carriage stopped at a *porte cochère*, and slowly drove through the gates into a paved square, Bertha could not repress her astonishment.

The old "Maison Brune"—for so it was named—formed three sides of a square. A low wall enabled you to see a terrace garden, that gradually sloped down to a tiny river, full of all that refreshing and gurgling sound peculiarly acceptable on a day so hot as this one was, and splashing its way over stones and pebbles, after the impetuous fashion of most small rivers.

"Is *this* our house?" exclaimed Bertha, in astonishment, as she descended from her exalted but lumbering vehicle, and gazed on the huge windows and large building before which she stood.

"It really is," said Frank, joyfully; "but come along," and as he spoke hastily mounting the two or three broad steps that led up to the front door. At the same moment the door was thrown wide open, and a trim little figure, in white jacket and cap, with a coloured woollen skirt and enormous earrings, appeared smiling a thousand unspoken welcomes.

"Jeanne," said Frank, by way of introduction, as he turned to assist Miss Thurston and the two little children.

Bertha, good humouredly, nodded to the little woman, leaving the question as to who she was for after investigation.

Entering the front door, Bertha found herself in a good sized square hall, panelled with oak; a large fireplace with iron dogs spoke of cheerful wood fires in winter. The floor was of polished oak, not (as in England) arranged in straight planks, so as to be as slippery and dangerous as possible—but inlaid and intersecting each other in a way that added considerably to the beauty of the effect and to everybody's safety. An old cabinet and a few high-backed chairs were all it boasted in the way of furniture. On one side of this hall were two good-sized rooms, one of which opened into a garden; and the same arrangement was carried out on the other side. Upstairs everything was equally lofty, airy, and spacious. No window-tax had contracted the size of the windows, and everything was beautifully and spotlessly clean.

The feeling of space was in itself delightful to Bertha, after the crowded inconveniences of the cottage and the little

London lodging; and, as she hastily made some arrangements for her children's comfort that night, she could hardly realize that her nurseries would now be so much after her own heart.

Miss Mary Thurston followed her about very much astonished at her satisfaction.

Realizing but faintly Bertha's past experiences, to *her* this large and bare-looking house formed a mournful contrast to the luxurious home of Bertha's girlhood, and she was fully prepared to exert her powers of condolence when she discovered they were not at all required.

She did every justice to the view, but she wished the lawn was smooth, instead of rough and neglected-looking grass; and she felt completely convinced that the thicket contained wolves!

To *her* eyes the oak panelling looked dull, and she would infinitely have preferred a light paper with a few roses, in odd posisitions, scattered over it.

When Bertha had completed her arrangements upstairs, she proclaimed herself exceedingly hungry, and quite ready to do justice to a sort of tea that Frank had ordered to be in readiness.

The ubiquitous Jeanne and Bertha were mutually pleased with each other, and it was settled that she should remain as their servant. She was the daughter of an old man, who acted as gardener and "odd-man" when the Maison Brune was inhabited, and who took care of the house when it was not.

"We must arrange to-morrow what rooms we shall absolutely require, and shut up all the others," said Frank that evening.

"Why?" asked Bertha, in astonishment.

"Because if we used the whole house we should require so many servants," he answered.

"In England, granted," said his wife, "but not abroad. No establishments abroad support dozens of servants to wait upon each other as we do in England. No, no; we will inhabit the house in all comfort; and Jeanne, and some one as cook, will be all we require."

A very tolerable cook is not a difficult matter to obtain abroad; and Jeanne introduced an active and elderly woman, who undertook all that was required, and who was especially delighted with her new mistress.

CHAPTER XXXV.

MADAME LA PRINCESSE DE SAUERLICH.

MISS THURSTON could not help wondering if she had been mistaken in Bertha's character all along. The quick and quiet way she had of disposing of a difficulty without disturbing her husband was no more than she might have expected her to do, but the practical good sense she showed in every possible way filled her with astonishment; and, as she watched her active helpfulness, she kept asking herself where the Bertha she remembered had gone.

Bertha, who at Haughton had lounged down to a late breakfast, and with whom she had had incessant skirmishes in her school-room days on that one point, was now up and all round the place; whilst Miss Mary was still adjusting, with methodical precision, the trim toilette in which she always appeared.

Through the day it was exactly the same thing. All the world knows the difference between work done with and without a will, and Miss Thurston remembered (with a regret that she was not there to see) Mrs. Borewell's prediction about Bertha's capabilities as a needlewoman.

At stated times the active fingers worked steadily, and the little repairs in her children's dress or her own were always exquisitely neat. They were beginning to feel a little at home now, and were sitting in the pleasant drawing-room one afternoon, waiting till the heat of the day lessened so as to enable them to go out, when the bell at the gate rang a sonorous peal.

Jeanne, having peeped into the room and nodded her appreciation of madame being "at home," opened the door and the gates, and a large and heavy coach, drawn by two very fat black horses, rolled into the yard.

It was Madame la Princesse de Sauerlich, her son, and M. l'Abbé Montmart, who held the position of half tutor and whole confessor to the Sauerlich family.

The princess was a short, fat, and good-natured-looking little woman, of middle age, dressed very dowdily, and panting from the extreme heat and the exertion of getting out of her carriage.

The prince was a heavy-looking young man, with a strong resemblance to his mother, and an air of phlegmatic dulness which she was without.

M. l'Abbé Montmart was a wizened-looking old Frenchman, with a sharp and inquisitive pair of eyes, that twinkled under the shadow of a pair of immensely thick and bushy eyebrows, and who took snuff perpetually in homœopathic portions at a time.

Bertha received her visitors with her

usual composed grace, and having introduced Miss Thurston, and been introduced to the two gentlemen, she sat down to diminish the distance between her height and that of the "great" lady.

The princess began by being dignified; she spoke very slowly, and inclined her head to one side in a way that rendered her very amusing. This assumption of dignity, however, was so foreign to her nature, that it soon evaporated, and Bertha found her just what she had expected, a good-humoured, shrewd little woman, commonplace, but not actually vulgar, and gifted with a large amount of curiosity.

She was evidently very much surprised at Bertha's appearance and manner, and kept looking at her cool muslin dress with a visible amount of envy. She was lost in admiration of the fair-haired children, and spoke warmly of the way in which Mr. Herbert had already shown his capabilities for business.

Miss Thurston, in the meantime, tried to engage the young prince in conversation, but found it a very difficult task—all the more so that his mother evidently took the entire management of his ideas into her own hands.

However much she appeared to be interested in the conversation she was carrying on with Bertha, her sharp ears overheard every word addressed to her son, and she answered the question for him, almost invariably addressing him as "my cabbage," in her very peculiar French accent, in which language the whole conversation was carried on.

The whole particulars of the remuneration for Miss Thurston's services, with the board she insisted on paying Bertha for her, she discussed openly, without the smallest reserve; and it is not quite certain whether Bertha or her friend felt most thoroughly uncomfortable. Bertha's sense of the ridiculous nearly overpowered her when the princess entered upon the subject of Miss Thurston's washing: but she managed to keep her countenance, and was relieved by the question started by M. l'Abbé, "If it rained, how was Miss Thurston to go to Sauerlich, and in deep snow?" Here was a subject for fresh discussion; but, as Madame de Sauerlich had a natural turn for arrangement, it was finally satisfactorily disposed of also.

These affairs settled, Madame de Sauerlich began to apologize to Bertha for the scanty furniture in the house, the draughts, the roughness of the garden, and many other things, and she assured Bertha that the pleasure of having obtained the services of so distinguished a gentleman as her husband was enhanced tenfold by the acquaintance and society of *so* charming a wife. She had always adored the English, and now she was quite enchanted to have secured such an acquisition to the society of the place.

Bertha assured her with great truth that she liked the place excessively, and thought she should be very happy. There was an unmistakable air of truth in Bertha's assertion, and the princess was delighted.

Having concluded what she termed *les affaires*, she gave Bertha a very amusing sketch of the neighbourhood; told her of the annual ball, which took place on the eve of the first hunting-day, and enlarged on the subject of the hunt, and the charming people it drew together—a subject which the young prince evidently took some interest in, for his countenance grew decidedly more animated than it had been hitherto.

When the princess finally took leave, she expressed a hope of seeing much of Bertha, explained the short cut through the grounds that Miss Thurston was to avail herself of daily, and cordially embraced "Madame Herbert" on both cheeks.

CHAPTER XXXVI.

THE TOWN OF DESSELDRINGEN AND ITS FAVOURITE PHYSICIAN.

DESSELDRINGEN was one of those small towns that resemble in many respects an overgrown English village. It had a curé, a bourguemestre (who was the leading spirit of the place), and several residents of moderate but comfortable fortunes.

The proximity of the château of Sauerlich, and the residence of the proprietors, gave Desseldringen aristocratic tendencies. It took a deep interest in Court news, a still deeper in the Sauerlich family, and considered itself entitled to hold its head considerably higher than neighbouring villages or towns that did not possess its great advantages.

There was a convent where some beautiful embroidery was done, which gave the nuns *one* interest in life, and a good deal of money; and there was last, not least, a doctor, who had once been a Hofrath, and who still retained the appellation.

The Doctor Knoplauch was a charming person altogether. Tall, broad-chested, and upright, he had completely that "*air noble*" that is in itself so fascinating. Guileless as a child, he was keen-witted, and had that indescribable something about him that checked presumption at once.

Slightly bald, his hair was a little longer than is usual, and his eyebrows were grey, and shaded a pair of very bright and intelligent blue eyes. His hands were very white and well-shaped, though large in proportion to his towering height (he was six feet two inches), and he was, in reality, very vain of them.

Bertha was perfectly delighted with him; she thought she had never met a more charming person; and there was something in his expression which so invited confidence, that she found herself talking to him with singular unreserve. Certainly, here was an acquaintance that at once made her feel "at home" in the place, and she sounded his praises so loudly to Miss Thurston and her husband, that the latter declared himself on the verge of jealousy. It is probable that Bertha, had she been planted at Desseldringen direct from Haughton, would have found nothing to interest her in the society of the place, and much to excite her propensity for turning everything into ridicule ; but, as it was, she saw so much to like in the genuine kind-heartedness of the people, that though she was often amused by their peculiarities, she did not despise them as she would certainly have done in former days, and she bent an attentive ear to trivial details that she would have, at one time of her life, treated loftily and scornfully.

There was something so limited in the interests of the little place, something so small in its views, that Miss Thurston fully expected that when the novelty of it all had worn off, Bertha would exclaim against its narrowness, and proclaim its insipidity. But day followed day, and no such signs appeared, and Miss Thurston admired Bertha much, and marvelled more at the way in which she continued to listen patiently to minute details, and even took an interest in them—stories of rival housekeepers, and constant disputes and complaints of the slowest of all slow diligences from the railway station; the one prominent anecdote of an upset and actually a broken arm; the cleverness of the Hofrath, and all the accompanying incidents, recounted with variations by every fresh acquaintance. Bertha listened with apparent sympathy, smiled, and shook her head exactly as she ought to have done. Nothing could have been more calculated to win the approbation of the Desseldringen society.

There was also a great charm to the innocent German fraus—who had arrived at a perfect knowledge of each other's cookery, and knew the mealy points of each other's domestic economy, who could name in a moment the housewife who inclined too much to vinegar, or too little to salt in her picklings—when they found a perfectly fresh listener, willing, nay eager, to profit by their experience, and who always accepted with gratitude a friendly hint about the management of her kitchen garden.

Frau Erlben, who was the excellent middle-aged wife of the "Ober post-master," delighted in Bertha's society, and gave her really a great many useful hints. How she knitted and how she talked! her knitting needles and her tongue kept pace together.

Her talk was harmless enough; indeed, the whole tone of the little place was innocence itself, and the only crimes quoted against any one there, was allowing a daughter too much liberty, or being indifferent to the management of one's house, dressing a little too gaily, or, perhaps, giving a dinner, with an attempt to outshine the other residents.

The fashion of society there was primitive and simple to a great degree.

Without counting the morning visits, which were frequent, stated invitations were occasionally sent out, when the invited guests arrived, armed with their work, or knitting, about four o'clock.

The young ladies of the house took off the cloaks, goloshes, &c., of the guests, and ushered them into the "salle," with an immense amount of ceremony. A sort of open tart, cut into slices and eaten like cake, was handed to each guest, with a glass of wine, also by the young ladies, and conversation and knitting flourished. By-and-by the tea was introduced—it was generally of a pale straw-colour, and, in every sense of the word, was the weakest part of the entertainment.

When the tea had been discussed, music generally followed, but it was not allowed to interrupt the conversation. The Germans having a knack of keeping up a subdued buzz, quite distinct to those close to each other, and yet not loud enough to disturb the performance, or those who draw near the piano to give their attention more fully to it.

Between nine and ten arrive the husbands and fathers, who have been cheerfully spending the evening either at the casino or a friend's house amidst clouds of smoke. Their arrival was the signal for departure, and a general shawling and cloaking process went on, and, with compliments begun in the drawing-room, on both sides, continuing all the way downstairs, and only concluding when the front door closed, the party broke up.

These *réunions* were amusing to Bertha; but, unfortunately, Frank did not "get on" with the Germans. In the first place, he found himself at a disadvantage from not knowing either French or German well enough to enter into the little jokes made; and if he accompanied Bertha to her "tea-parties" he was equally out of his element. Altogether, this life abroad suited her infinitely better than it did him; and Bertha often felt a pang of regret as she saw how completely he was lost away from England. The reflection that, but for *her* relation's dishonesty, this exile would have been unnecessary was the only drawback to a life in which she thankfully acknowledged the chief element of happiness—peace.

CHAPTER XXXVII.

A HUNT BALL.

Time passed on, as it usually does, with greater swiftness, apparently, where all is so monotonous; and the month of October had arrived.

Two great events formed prominent subjects of conversation at Desseldringen.

The hunt ball was to be on an unusual scale of splendour, as a marriage in the royal family had called for some demonstrations of loyalty; and Desseldringen turned over in its own mind how best it could keep up its superiority over the surrounding towns, with a due regard, in the first place, to its funds—in the second, to its capabilities.

No one knew from whence they received the suggestion, but it was decided, in the first place, that the corporation would give the ball, instead of allowing it to be merely one of subscription, as was usually the case; and it was also decided that the town should be illuminated. Various other things were to be done, for the poor especially, who were well cared for by the good people of the place.

The other great topic was the probable presence of a German prince of the blood royal, who was to be in the neighbourhood, and had half promised to attend.

To Bertha the idea of any ball's creating so much excitement was most amusing; her simple but pretty style of dress had created so much admiration, that she was invaded at all hours by anxious mothers, and no less anxious daughters, beseeching her to give them one word of advice upon this all-important subject. Fair and rather stout *mädchen*, with a profusion of flaxen hair, proposed the most *outré* style of dress, as represented in the distorted figures of a French fashion-book; and it is almost needless to say, that in hardly any one instance was Bertha's advice followed.

Bertha had represented so strongly to Miss Thurston the drawback her absence would be to her engagement, that the little woman had consented to accompany her; and when the evening arrived, Frank, who thought it a bore, but was glad his wife should have any amusement, escorted the two ladies to the ball.

"To the left, my dear Frau Herbert—to the left," exclaimed the Frau Erlben, as the party from the Maison Brune descended at the door of the court-house, and found themselves in a brilliantly-lighted entrance hall, where a band of music was playing with all the sweetness of a really good German band.

"To the left" was a cloak-room, and as Bertha threw off her wraps a murmur of admiration ran through the room. She had on her wedding dress (white satin, very slightly trimmed with blonde), a small diamond star in her hair, and a tiny ornament round her throat. Her skin looked perfectly dazzling to the admiring German eyes.

She was warmly greeted by those she knew, and was proceeding to the ball-room with her husband and Miss Thurston, when her steps were arrested by an anxious voice pronouncing her name.

"Pardon me, dear Frau Herbert," said Frau Erlben, breathlessly, "but your scarf —you have forgotten your scarf."

"My scarf!" echoed Bertha; "I have not got any; I never wear such a thing."

"Never wear a scarf!" said Frau Erlben in astonishment; "but you cannot go into a ball-room without a scarf!"

"Why not?" asked Bertha, in astonishment; "because—because," and the excellent woman lowered her voice so that

Frank could not hear, "it would be considered so immodest."

"What, not to wear a scarf?" said Bertha; "what utter nonsense!" and she attempted to move on.

"Pray take mine," said the good-natured Frau, throwing a dingy gauze enormity over Bertha's lovely dress; "I will get another for myself."

Frank's patience utterly deserted him. "For my sake, shake her and it off," he whispered, with a look of disgust at the offending article of dress.

Bertha took it off, saying—"I am English, and will follow the English customs, which do not make this necessary." She handed it to the discomfited frau and passed on.

If Bertha had expected to pass unnoticed into the ball-room, she was extremely in the wrong.

In a London ball-room, she was on a par with a good many other women, who were handsome and well-dressed; *here* she was so much handsomer than any one in the room, that the Princesse von Sauerlich came forward to claim her immediately, feeling what a prestige her presence gave to her party. The grand duke, for the grand duke *was* there, was immensely struck, and begged to place himself at her feet immediately; several of the members of the hunt were of course immensely struck also, and Frank was considerably amused at the sensation his wife created.

It is not to be supposed, in the meantime, that the excellent German ladies saw this success without making their own comments upon it.

"How the Engländerian can allow those gentlemen to monopolize her in that way, *I* cannot think!" said one.

"And to think of her coming into the room with those naked shoulders!" said another; "the English books tell us of the way in which the English ladies behave in private life; and if they do all that they are *said* to do, no wonder they think nothing of coming into a room half-dressed."

"English society is at a very low ebb, indeed," remarked the wife of the professor of English, in the academy, who was supposed to be thoroughly acquainted with the literature, manners and customs of the English. "It is a perfectly ascertained fact that the women in good society marry two and sometimes three husbands; they run away with other people's husbands, and they push them down wells when they get tired of them; they marry their grooms and do all sorts of dreadful things, not proper to be spoken about before tender young plants," and she drew herself up and looked affectionately at a young scion of English professorship at her side.

"Herr, Je!" exclaimed several voices.

"Frau Herbert does not look capable of much wickedness, Frau Semmling," said the kindly and sonorous voice of the Hofrath.

"Ah! Herr Hofrath, I did not know you were there," exclaimed the professor's wife, who had a wholesome feeling of respect for him, as the only person she was a little afraid of.

"I do not think you did know it," he replied; "so Frau Herbert is supposed to have murdered several husbands and married her groom, because she does not choose to disfigure herself with a stupid thing like this," and he touched the end of the Frau Semmling's scarf as he spoke.

"When people have come to reside in a country, they should adopt the manners and customs of that country, and not offend people's prejudices," answered Frau Semmling, with great dignity.

"Humph!" said Herr Hofrath, calmly; "then you see one can hardly call this small town of ours *a country*, it is merely a provincial town, in a rather out-of-the-way part of the world; people would have enough to do if they adopted the peculiar notions of every small town in which they happened to reside."

"It *may* be a provincial town as you say," said the Frau Semmling, who was getting very indignant; "but when royalty is present, it seems to me a little respect would not be out of place."

"Royalty does not seem to take exception at Frau Herbert's English ways," said the Hofrath, looking as he spoke at the deferential attitude of the great man who was in close conversation with Bertha.

"Bah!" said the Frau Semmling, who rose with a jerk, and proceeded to another part of the room with her young daughter.

The Hofrath smiled and looked round the room as if in search of somebody, and slowly he made his way through the throng of people, and sat down by the side of Miss Mary Thurston.

The fashion of the balls at Desseldringen was as follows:—After the Sauerlich party had danced a "Française" (which one may mention to the unenlightened is simply an old-fashioned English quadrille), the band struck up the next dance, generally a waltz, and then stopped for some time.

The master of the ceremonies, with much politeness and many bows, indicated to the dancers where they had better stand; for a waltz, the ladies stood in a row with their backs to the wall, and their partners faced them, as if a country-dance was going to be danced. When all was ready, the master of the ceremonies made a signal with his hand, and the band began to play again.

The master of the ceremonies walked gravely down by the side of as many couple as he considered the room would conveniently accommodate, and those started and waltzed so many times round the room, returning to their places. When they had finished, he started the next number of dancers in the same way, and so on till the dance ended.

The Germans (who have an idea that no

one can dance but themselves) were extremely surprised when they saw Bertha's graceful movements. She danced with the grand duke, and he was so delighted with her, that he confided to his aide-de-camp that she was the most beautiful woman and the best dancer he had ever met, and he hoped that she would appear at the hunt meet next morning, and look as well by daylight as she did at night; an opinion and hope the aide-de-camp thought right to convey to all the acquaintances he had, and which did not tend to increase Bertha's waning popularity.

END OF VOL. I.

www.ingramcontent.com/pod-product-compliance
Lightning Source LLC
Chambersburg PA
CBHW030811230426
43667CB00008B/1161